MORAL THEOLOGY

A Reader

Edited by Patrick Hannon

MORAL THEOLOGY

A Reader

Edited by Patrick Hannon

First published 2006 by
Veritas Publications
7/8 Lower Abbey Street
Dublin 1, Ireland
Email publications@veritas.ie
Website www.veritas.ie

ISBN 1 85390 962 9

'Five Ways of Looking at Morality' by Donal Harrington from *What is Morality?*, courtesy of Columba Press, 1996, pp. 9–27. 'Is There a Natural Law?' by Donal Harrington from *What is Morality?*, courtesy of Columba Press, 1996, pp. 95–112. 'Approaching Christian Morality' by Vincent MacNamara, courtesy of *The Furrow*, April 1997, pp. 213–220. 'Christian Faith and Morality' by Vincent MacNamara, courtesy of *The Furrow*, January 1984 (15). 'Forming and Following One's Conscience' by Linda Hogan, courtesy of *Doctrine and Life,* September 1993, pp. 402–410. 'Justifying Moral Positions' by Vincent MacNamara, courtesy of *The Furrow*, September 1978, pp. 560–568. 'Moral Character' by Bill Cosgrave, courtesy of *The Furrow*, January 2000, pp. 24–33. 'Can Goodness Be Taught?' by Pádraig Hogan, courtesy of *The Furrow*, February 1989, pp. 90–98 (revised). 'Sin and Sinfulness' by Hugh Connolly from *Sin*, courtesy of Continuum Press, 2002. 'A Feminist Approach to Sin' by Elizabeth Rees, courtesy of *The Furrow*, December 1999, pp. 647–654. 'HIV and Catholic Theology' by Julie Clague, courtesy of CAFOD website:
www.cafod.org.uk/resources/worship/theological_articles/living_positively

A catalogue record for this book
is available from the British Library.

Cover design by Niamh McGarry
Printed in the Republic of Ireland
by Betaprint Ltd.

Veritas books are printed on paper made from the wood pulp of managed forests. For every tree felled, at least one tree is planted, thereby renewing natural resources.

CONTENTS

CONTRIBUTORS

Julie Clague is Lecturer in Catholic Theology at the University of Glasglow. She is a member of the Theological Commission of Caritas and works as a theologian with the Catholic international aid agencies CAFOD and SCIAF.

Hugh Connolly is Vice-President and Lecturer in Moral Theology at Maynooth. He is the author of *Sin* (London/New York: Continuum (New Century series) 2002).

Bill Cosgrave is Parish Priest of Monageer, Co. Wexford. A collection of his essays in moral and pastoral theology entitled *Christian Living Today* was published by Columba Press in 2001.

Donal Harrington has lectured in Moral Theology in Mater Dei Institute, Dublin and in Carlow College. He writes on parish renewal and development as well as on moral theology. The chapters included in this collection are from his *What is Morality? The Light Through Different Windows* (Dublin: Columba Press, 1995).

Linda Hogan is Professor and Head of the Irish School of Ecumenics, Trinity College, Dublin. She is the author of

Confronting the Truth: Conscience in the Catholic Tradition (New York: Paulist Press, 2000).

Pádraig Hogan lectures in Education at the National University of Ireland, Maynooth. He is author of *The Custody and Courtship of Experience: Western Education in Philosophical Perspective* (Dublin: Columba Press, 1995).

Vincent MacNamara lectures at Milltown Institute, Dublin. His most recent book is *New Life for Old: On Desire and Becoming Human* (Dublin: Columba Press, 2004).

Elizabeth Rees OCV is Director of a House of Prayer in rural Somerset. She lectures in Early Church History and Celtic Studies, and leads retreats.

INTRODUCTION

—— Patrick Hannon ——

When people talk about moral matters – the rights and wrongs of a war, say, or honesty in politics, or sexual fidelity, or human rights – some words and expressions are likely to recur. One such word is *conscience*, as when it is said that support for a war is a 'question of conscience'; or that it's 'up to your conscience' to decide whether to blow the whistle on a scam at work; or that 'my conscience is troubling me' over money I took from a friend one time; or that a ruler who authorises torture 'has no conscience'.

Another term is *principle*, as when we say that keeping your word is 'a matter of principle', or that so-and-so is a 'person of principle', or that I refuse to buy something which is the product of slave labour 'on principle'. Yet another term is *value*, meaning something – an attitude, perhaps, or a way of acting, or a quality, held to be important – truthfulness, say, or trust, or fidelity, or having a care for people who have no-one to look after them.

And of course there is the word *moral* itself, and *morality* and *immorality*, and, now often used instead, *ethical* and *unethical* and *ethics*. Both of these sets of words have roots in the idea of 'the way things are done' (*mores, ethos*), by 'rational' people, or those who know right from wrong, or perhaps just 'good' people. But the words are not merely descriptive. The way things are done by people who know right from wrong, or who deserve to be called good, is also the way things *ought* to be done.

If the people talking about moral questions – what's right and wrong, good and bad, what ought to be done – come from a religious background, the chances are that their ideas are influenced by the religion of their home or school or place of worship. So influential are the religious traditions, indeed, that people often think of moral values and principles as religious, as a matter of God's 'law', or 'the will of God', or as what's wanted if we 'love' God. Some religious people are disconcerted by the suggestion that it could be otherwise, that there are men and women who live good lives, who are honest, just, kind, unselfish, even though they profess no religious faith at all.

Of course it's not long since members of the Christian Churches had a problem with the notion that members of another Christian Church might be as good-living or better than themselves. And what Christians made of the morals of followers of the other two religions of the Book may be glimpsed in such relatively 'innocent' creations as the character of Shylock in Shakespeare's *Merchant of Venice*, or in *King Lear*'s Edgar's words, 'Wine loved I deeply, dice dearly, and in woman out-paramoured the Turk'.

Nowadays, it is true, the Churches are bidden to recognise their common Christian inheritance, and to see the good in the ways of other faiths and of other people of good will. But some Christians will continue to feel uneasy when morality is talked about as 'a human thing', or as though you don't need religion to know about it, or in a way which doesn't immediately link it to the Bible or the teaching of Jesus Christ. And some Church people will be dismayed by talk about morality which seems to make little of Church authority.

But it is also true that the authority of Church teaching and teachers has weakened, as contemporary western culture calls into question the truth claims of religious tradition, even as it accentuates the values associated with economic progress, personal freedom and individual entitlement. And, locally and globally, concrete moral questions multiply, arising from technological advances, for example, or from new political configurations, or changing economic and social circumstances. In the absence of a sense of the security that goes with belonging to a centuries-long tradition, many people are bewildered.

The changed scene is perhaps especially problematic for people of a Catholic background, inasmuch as it has been characteristic of Catholic teaching to stress both the moral aspects of the Christian faith and the teaching authority of the Church's *magisterium*, the Pope and the bishops. There is no need for detail here as regards the 'crisis of authority', which has afflicted the Church for four decades, nor is there scope to explore the apparent ambivalence whereby Pope John Paul II is praised for his leadership on social justice and human rights by many who have rejected his teaching on sexuality. In general it can be said that though the profile of, especially, papal magisterium remains high, and the lines of moral doctrine remain clear, the questioning of elements of the Catholic tradition has persisted, even among Catholics themselves.

Catholic teaching about morality is to be found in the *Catechism of the Catholic Church*. 'Life in Christ' is the title of Part Three, and it offers a vision of the human, and of human possibility, which is summarised in an early paragraph.

The dignity of the human person is rooted in his creation in the image and likeness of God; it is fulfilled in his vocation to divine beatitude. It is essential to a human being freely to direct himself to this fulfilment. By his deliberate actions, the human person does, or does not, conform to the good promised by

God and attested by moral conscience. Human beings make their own contribution to their interior growth; they make their whole sentient and spiritual lives into means of this growth. With the help of grace they grow in virtue, avoid sin, and if they sin they entrust themselves as did the prodigal son to the mercy of our Father in heaven. In this way they attain to the perfection of charity (1700).

The meaning of this is unfolded in what follows, and the concrete requirements for living in accordance with the Christian vision are set forth in an account of each of the Ten Commandments, seen in terms of the core commandment of Jesus' teaching: love of God and neighbour.

What the *Catechism* provides is both the culmination and the starting-point of a study of the central and characteristic insights of the Catholic moral tradition. It is a culmination, for it is the fruit of experience and reflection, but it may also be a starting-point, for it will prompt questions too. Inevitably, not all the questions which a reader may have, in the form in which he or she may have them, are answered here, especially for someone not already schooled in the terminology of theological or philosophical thinking, or not already at home in what St Paul called the household of the faith.

All this by way of prelude to a selection of readings from Catholic moral theology which, apart from one, deal not in the first place with particular and concrete moral issues but with the kind of question adverted to at the outset, basic or fundamental questions which underlie discussion of any and all concrete issues. For that kind of question – where do values and norms come from? why should we be moral? where does our religion come in? – emerges if we reflect for a while on any of the concrete problems.

Take euthanasia, for example. Catholic Church teaching is that this is indeed a question of conscience in the sense that it's a moral question, a question of medical ethics, but that it's not up to your conscience or mine to decide on euthanasia's rightness, for it is seen as the 'direct' taking of a life and so is wrong. Why accept this teaching? Does it stand to reason, and if it does, how come some reasonable people think differently? So does it depend on 'faith', on the acceptance of a special revelation about what God's design for humans is? If so, where is this revelation found? In the Bible, accepted by all Christians as the word of God? So how can there be differences about euthanasia among Christians? Or about abortion, or capital punishment, or warfare?

Five Ways of Looking at Morality

Some of the differences on practical questions arise because of differences in the way people look at morality itself, and Donal Harrington has identified five such ways. In the first chapter he shows how each of the ways is likely to shape our thinking. Do you think of morality the way you think of *law*, as something imposed, perhaps under threat of punishment, or do you think of it in terms of *inner conviction*, or of *love*? Is becoming good the same as, or related to, *personal growth*? Does morality arise only with the various particular, mostly individual, relationships in which we find ourselves, as parent or partner, daughter or son, employer or employee, client or professional – or does it also have to do with *social transformation*, with trying to change for the better the society in which we live, with contributing to the building up of community? Is any of these perspectives predominant, or is any one or more of them absent from my idea of what morality is? The answers that I give to such questions will tell something about the kind of person I am and how I live my daily life.

The title of Donal Harrington's second chapter, asking whether there is a natural law, is a question that arises from a number of points of view. It arises when people say that you don't need religion to have a moral code, because what's right and wrong can be worked out by reason reflecting on human nature or experience; or when this is contested on the basis that there's no such thing as human nature in the abstract, and that human experience varies as between one period of history and another and between different cultures. It arose dramatically after World War II when those who participated in Nazi atrocities tried to defend themselves by saying that they were only obeying orders. And it sometimes lurks under the surface when human rights are argued about, including particular rights such as the right to life or the right to a fair trial. Catholic teaching has always said there is a natural law, and Harrington explains why and how an account of natural law might meet the difficulties which emerge when you start to think it through.

One of these is that it seems much more obvious and attractive for a Christian to look to the person and teaching of Christ for guidance on how to live. Jesus taught that 'all the Law and the Prophets' come down to the love-commandment, something that had already been indicated in the Law and by Old Testament prophets themselves. Jesus made it clear too, though, that he wasn't setting aside the Commandments of the first Covenant; it remains wrong to murder and steal and commit adultery, for example, and to neglect or oppress the poor. But Jesus reminds his hearers that it is wrong also to hate or lust or covet riches, or to succumb to hardness of heart. New Testament writings take up the idea of a 'new covenant', indeed a 'new creation', a new 'life in the Spirit', discipleship and imitation of Christ, the kingdom or rule of the God of loving-kindness and justice and peace.

All of this is surely more engaging and enlivening than talk of a natural law, a law of nature, especially when there seems to be a lack of clarity as to what this law requires, or when what the term suggests is, in Tennyson's memorable phrase, 'nature red in tooth and claw'. One of the criticisms of the moral theology of the textbooks which dominated Catholic theology from the beginning of the seventeenth century until the middle of the twentieth was that the picture of morality which they drew showed little sign of the vision of the Scriptures, was indeed no more than 'a version of natural law'. There are Christians for whom the Bible is as it were the last word – the literal sense of its texts is taken as normative. But even mainstream Christian thinking, including especially the theology of what is called the renewal of Catholic moral theology, insists on the need to be informed by biblical insight and perspective if one is to have an understanding of the moral life which is truly Christian.

It must seem then that to speak of morality as a human experience common to people of every and no religion is from a Christian point of view at best something of a digression. Yet, as both of Donal Harrington's essays indicate, there are dangers in too hasty an account of it in religious terms, and in some of the models of its relation to religious faith which are to be found even in the biblical material itself. No good is done to our understanding of either morality or religion – not to mention our relationship to people not of the faith – if we fail to give the general human experience of morality its due weight. And, granted all that is at stake, for good and ill, in 'globalisation' and 'pluralism', and in the possibilities for good and ill with which modern 'progress' confront the race, it would be folly to ignore the commonalities of human experience, or to abandon the prospect of at least a common language of morality such as can be glimpsed still in the ancient notion of a natural law.

Approaching Christian Morality

This is part of the importance of Vincent MacNamara's first piece, which sketches an 'approach' to a Christian understanding that emphasises that morality is both a fact of universal human experience and a matter of reason, that its requirements can be rationally defended and its 'point' accounted for without reference to religious belief. God is no more the author of the principles of morality than of the principles of logic, he says, startlingly perhaps, especially for a reader used to thinking in terms of God's Law and the Commandments, and eternal reward and punishment.

MacNamara is not going to say that God has nothing to do with the difference between good and evil, or with our obligation to do good, and in the next reading he explores in detail the differences which Christian faith makes. But he is at pains now to ensure that we don't think of God's 'role' (if one can so speak) as like that of a garda or a high court judge or even a legislator. God is the author of creation, including the human in creation, and humans have the God-given power of reason by which they can discover and apply the principles of logic – and the principles of morality.

At this point we may recall what the *Catechism* says: 'The dignity of the human person is rooted in his creation in the image and likeness of God; it is fulfilled in his vocation to divine beatitude. It is essential to a human being freely to direct himself to this fulfilment. By his deliberate actions, the human person does, or does not, conform to the good promised by God and attested by moral conscience.' MacNamara's reflections have put us on notice that *beatitudo*, Aquinas' rendering of Aristotle's word *eudaimonia* – happiness, fulfilment, flourishing – is not at odds with what is human but enhances it immeasurably. As to what is right and wrong conduct, what counts as good living, faith in the God of Jesus

Christ is not at odds with reason. And in a Christian vision, in the words of second-century theologian St Irenaeus, the glory of God is humanity 'fully alive'.

So in what way is the search for the right way to live illumined by the light of faith in the Gospel, the 'good news' enabled and attested in the life, death and resurrection of Jesus of Nazareth? The starting-point of MacNamara's 'Christian Faith and Morality' is the point at which the first piece concludes. For all that there is a core to the experience of morality which may be recognised by people of no particular religious allegiance and people of other faiths, the Christian sees the moral life also in ways that are different, and MacNamara identifies and explains the chief of these.

There is the Christian understanding of *eudaimonia* as *beatitudo*, in the end the vision of God and a sharing in God's life, of which we could not know if God had not revealed it. But other truths emerge also out of the experience of God's self-disclosure in the history of the people of the Covenant, and in the person and word and works of Jesus Christ. What these are, and how they bear upon our understanding of morality and our efforts at living this out, is conveyed in the living tradition of the community we call church. Vincent MacNamara' second piece in this collection intimates ways in which the life and worship of that community may afford a glimpse of 'the breadth and length and height and depth' of which Paul writes in the third chapter of the letter to the Ephesians, and of the ways in which Christian perspectives may form and inform the conscience.

Conscience
The topic of conscience has arisen in each of the preceding readings, and it is mentioned in the paragraph from the *Catechism* quoted above. A later paragraph says: 'Conscience is

a judgment of reason whereby the human person recognises the moral quality of a concrete act that he is going to perform, is in the process of performing, or has already completed. In all he says and does, man is obliged to follow faithfully what he knows to be just and right. It is by the judgment of his conscience that man perceives and recognises the prescriptions of the divine law' (1778). Later again we are told: 'A human being must always obey the certain judgment of his conscience. If he were deliberately to act against it, he would condemn himself' (1790).

Plainly conscience is of the first importance, and the ultimacy of conscience judgment here affirmed sounds a note heard as early as St Paul's Letter to the Romans and resonating in Aquinas and Newman and the Second Vatican Council. The assertion raises questions of course, some of which are immediately met by other observations of the Catechism. 'Yet it can happen that moral conscience remains in ignorance and makes erroneous judgments about acts to be performed or already committed', paragraph 1790 continues. And this ignorance 'can often be imputed to personal responsibility. This is the case when a man or woman 'takes little trouble to find out what is true and good, or when conscience is by degrees almost blinded through the habit of committing sin'. In such cases, the person is culpable for the evil he commits' (1791, quoting Vatican II).

• More positively, 'conscience must be informed and moral judgment enlightened. A well-formed conscience is upright and truthful. It formulates its judgments according to reason, in conformity with the true good willed by the wisdom of the Creator. The education of conscience is indispensable for human beings who are subjected to negative influences and tempted by sin to prefer their own judgment and to reject authoritative teachings' (1783). The education of conscience is a life-long process (1784), and 'in the formation of conscience the Word of God is the light for our path, we must assimilate it in faith and prayer and put it into practice. We must also examine our conscience before the Lord's Cross. We are assisted by the gifts of the Holy Spirit, aided by the witness or advice of others and guided by the authoritative teaching of the Church' (1785). And 'it is important for every person to be sufficiently present to himself in order to hear and follow the voice of his conscience. This requirement of *interiority* is all the more necessary as life often distracts us from any reflection, self-examination or introspection' (1779).

Forming and following one's conscience is the subject of Linda Hogan's contribution, and she is conscious of ambiguities which surfaced in some public debate about moral matters in Ireland in the closing years of the last century. Specifically, 'while on the one hand, personal responsibility is both recognised and valued, on the other there seems to be a desire for certainty and simplicity'. Hogan reports the experience of teachers of religion: 'while young adults frequently voice disagreement with traditional magisterial teaching, particularly on issues pertaining to sexual morality, they still look for ready-made answers to the moral complexities of our day.' This article was written in the early nineties but one has the impression that the situation hasn't greatly changed; and the yearning for certainty and simplicity is not confined to young adults.

All of the earlier readings touch on the difficulty of achieving clarity in the application of principles to concrete situations, a difficulty adverted to by St Thomas Aquinas in these very terms, and by Aristotle when he warned against expecting from moral judgment the clarity associated with mathematics. Tracing the history of the concept of conscience and of the Christian theological tradition concerning its role, Linda Hogan's article focuses on the problems that arise when simple answers to complex questions are expected, and on some of the ways in which such difficulties might be met. She is very aware of what has come to be called 'dissent' in the Church, a questioning by the faithful or by theologians of moral teaching on sexuality, say, or certain questions in bioethics. Without denying that moral blindness or obtuseness can derive from the kind of causes of which the *Catechism* speaks, her particular concern is with obstacles to moral maturity that are rooted in naive conceptions of the role of the Bible or of Church tradition, or in childish expectations of authority.

Justifying Moral Positions

Similar concerns, though from a different starting-point, emerge in Vincent MacNamara's 'Justifying Moral Positions'. Nobody needs reminding, he writes, that people are daily less inclined to accept directives without explanation. 'They have learned to question established teaching in many areas of life, to reject some of the old answers, and to expect new insights. They likewise question moral positions. So, the community must examine how it engages in the business of morality. A failure to produce reasons leads to the suspicion that moral positions cannot be justified. A fear that we cannot justify them leads to a defensiveness, that can be mistaken for arrogance or lack of understanding, and that destroys the possibility of dialogue or real education'.

By community MacNamara means the Christian community in particular, though as in the other chapters he is conscious of commonalities in human experience, as well as what looks different when seen through a Christian lens. As before and like the other authors he takes Aristotle's and Aquinas' point about the complexity of concrete moral choice. He acknowledges that the Christian Church or churches have a position on many matters of moral concern: 'Do not steal, or kill, or commit adultery or abortion, or injure another, or engage in pre-marital sex, or break promises, or slander another, or divorce your spouse.' Such statements do aid moral judgment, and their basis and significance can and should be presented in Christian moral education. But it would be wrong, Vincent MacNamara says, to think of the task of the moral educator as simply one of issuing statements of this kind. 'Even if we had hundreds of them, they would not absolve the individual from the call to grapple with his very personal situation, to assess its particularity and to respond to it as fully and as responsibly as possible. They would not substitute for the heart-searching and the sensitivity to persons and situations that conscience-decision requires.'

Moral Character and the Education in Virtue
Prohibitions such as those just listed have their importance in the process of coming to a right moral judgment, the judgment as to what I ought to do or not, as have more positive precepts, such that we should keep our word, and tell the truth, and pay what we owe, and the like. But we shall not use them wisely (or indeed at all) unless we have a mind for it, as the saying goes. By that I mean first having a *mentality* or general *attitude* which respects other people and wants to give them their rights and respond to their needs as called to, a *will* to do them good. But it means also, secondly, having the *capacity* to translate this mentality or attitude or will into *action*. That capacity involves not only the *knowledge* of moral principle or norm or rule – a knowledge, say, of the Ten Commandments – but also the *wisdom* to discern what is asked of us in the unfolding story of our lives.

  Aristotle said that justice is not only the doing of just actions but the doing of them in the way of the just person. That means behaving out of a right intention and motive and attitude, and with a general disposition to justice. And a disposition to justice or any other form of goodness, translated into practice, leads to a certain ease of performance. Someone who possesses the appropriate 'art' will be observed to play golf or swim or sing or paint with a kind of fluency. And so it is with morals: disposition translates into habit, and habit tends toward facility, and we develop a 'style', characteristic ways of behaving which are part of our make-up.

This kind of point is in various ways in each of the readings so far, but it is central to Bill Cosgrave's piece on 'Character'. This shows how our moral choices shape and form our moral character even as our character gives rise to and conditions our choices. There is a reciprocal relationship: 'by acting in certain ways consistently we make ourselves to be certain sorts of persons, either for good or for evil. On the other hand, who we are now as persons powerfully influences and conditions what we choose to do or not do.'

Thus if someone acts generously often and over a long period, he or she is not just expressing a generosity but is in an important sense 'becoming' a generous person. We would say that that person has or is a generous 'character', has the 'virtue' of generosity. Similarly of course with a vice such as stinginess or laziness. 'The other side of this coin is that one who is a just person will usually act in a just way, while one who is intemperate will usually behave intemperately.' Cosgrave draws attention to the word 'usually': few people, if any, are always generous or mean or lazy, most act in those ways only most of the time, and even the best of people sometimes act out of character.

Evidently, then, says Cosgrave, 'there is some good in the worst of us and some bad in the best of us'. And there can be degrees of goodness and badness in one's character: 'some are very good (or bad) indeed, while others are clearly less consistently good (or bad). It even seems the case that some haven't as yet determined a direction in their way of choosing and so let the direction vary from one decision to another.' These ideas lead directly to the next three readings, for they raise the question of moral failure, of sin as it is called in theology, and they may lead us to wonder whether or how goodness can be taught.

● 'Can goodness be taught?' is precisely the question which Pádraig Hogan puts himself, a question which must resonate with parent and teacher and pastor or anyone whose calling brings responsibility in the moral education of the young. Hogan writes out of a keen awareness of the changes that have taken place so swiftly in Irish society, challenging the *mores* of generations of a religiously-minded people, displacing received authority in matters of morality as of religion, and posing drastic questions for the future of moral education in Church and school and home.

But he reminds us that these problems and challenges are not without precedent; a sentence from Martin Buber's 1930s essay 'The Education of Character' sounds a note heard elsewhere in the pages of this reader: 'to deny the presence of universal values and norms of absolute validity – that is the conspicuous tendency of our age.' And Hogan recalls that the question of his title perplexed the ancient Greeks. Still, the conditions of the question are new in Ireland, and the question has acquired a particular urgency here.

The teaching of religion and morality at post-primary level is Pádraig Hogan's special concern in this reading. A central contention is that● 'Goodness *can* be learned, *is* continually being learned *and* unlearned, in the everyday experiences of being human in a world shared with others. If we could understand better how teaching, rather than frustrate or take custody of such unforced learning, could turn it to more fruitful purpose, we should have made a significant advance in pursuing our question'. A critical factor, in his view, is the need to distinguish between an educational interest in moral or religious tradition, and interests which are 'evangelical' or 'institutional'. He explains how this might be done and what the consequences would be, and he sketches possibilities which are heartening in terms of any of the interests.

Sin and Sinfulness

Whatever the possibilities of teaching goodness we need not expect the disappearance of moral failure, and in a book on the basics of a Christian understanding of morality it would be strange if we were to omit consideration of sin. It is a common complaint that Catholic theology has tended to be pre-occupied with sin, and there is truth in the complaint, though it is sometimes overstated, and it is arguable that some modern moral theology hasn't taken this side of experience seriously enough.

Christian theology, though with varying emphases as between traditions, has always understood the human heart as torn between a desire for God and a self-love which is ultimately destructive, and it is to this condition that the Gospel speaks. A consciousness of the sin which is abroad in the world, a sinfulness which awaits us as we enter the world, which seems to have taken hold of the very structures of human existence, moves in the direction of a doctrine of 'original sin'. But – unless we are deluded – we become conscious also of 'actual sin', that which free human action perpetrates, the way in which men and women miss the mark, to use a biblical expression, preferring the semblance of good to the true good.

There have been – and are – understandings of sin which have made a monster of God, or a delinquent child of the creature said in the Book of Genesis to be made in God's image.

Other accounts have made it seem that sin is failure in interpersonal relationship only, and not when we fail to recognise our indebtedness to human community, or when we fail in care of the world which we inhabit. Christian theology has not always appreciated the reality of what St Paul called the 'sin of the world', or the possibility of what some theologians call 'social sin', or the ways in which society fails or further wounds the vulnerable.

Modern theologies try to do better, sometimes by recovering biblical and other early perspectives, sometimes by 'contextualising' theological thinking, sometimes with the aid of the human sciences; though it would be folly to think that we are now getting it completely right. Hugh Connolly's chapter recounts the fortunes of understandings of sin and sinfulness, historically and in modern writing; and his appraisal includes indications of the requirements of a better approach.

Of the voices in modern theology which are especially important in the search for a better approach, Connolly mentions the contributions of those who write from political, ecological, liberationist and feminist perspectives. The work of these writers has in fact been influential more generally in moral theology, including as regards a basic understanding of the moral life, as may be gathered from almost all of the other readings. Hence the choice of the two final chapters in this collection, each of which is important not only because of its subject matter but also for its methodology.

Elizabeth Rees writes of sin and related themes also, but from an avowedly feminist standpoint. Her experience, candidly recounted, painful sometimes to read, is the experience of a woman, and it speaks to women's experience – though perhaps to some men too. She writes of course of the sins of the patriarchy, of the persistent fact that women are sinned against in Church and society. But critique is not the point of her reflection; she is in search of a way to understand basic themes of the Christian account of what we are and what we are called to be.

A striking thought, one of many: 'Women know what it feels like to "bear the sins of the world": the tired mother who answers her crying baby night after night, the single parent who goes without necessities so that her children can eat enough, the wife raped by her husband, the woman who sells her body to pay school fees. These women share in the action of Jesus, the Lamb of God, who bears the sin of the world. Women who struggle to bring life to a Church which tells them: "Go away!" – these women are helping God to redeem the world; they are giving birth to a new creation of love and freedom. These women know sin, because they are engaged in redeeming the world.'

Spiritual insight out of mundane and horrific and sordid experiences, but insights too from old and modern guides. Thomas Merton is an unsurprising mentor to a modern woman or man, but Rees is indebted also to Syriac scholarship and the theology of Ephraem the Syrian – and of course the Christian and Hebrew scriptures.

Moral Theology Applied: the HIV/AIDS Pandemic

The Hebrew and Christian scriptures provide the starting-point of Julie Clague's essay, as she brings a 'liberationist' perspective to bear on the HIV/AIDS pandemic. Some versions of liberation theology drew Vatican disapproval in the 1980s, mainly because they were seen as infected by an unacceptable Marxism. But it is possible to acknowledge the merits of a liberationist approach, for – in line with some Old Testament orientations – 'the whole of Jesus' ministry can be viewed as one of liberating people from sin, healing the sick and repairing brokenness. It is given classical expression in Matthew's

Sermon on the Mount and Luke's Sermon on the Plain. It is clear that the priorities of the reign of God are the concerns of the sick and hungry before the comfortable and wealthy.

The Second Vatican Council reiterated these priorities, and it adverted also to the social character of sin. This means that, as Clague puts it, 'humans are born into and conditioned by their sinful surrounds. There is systemic and structural injustice, political and economic corruption that distorts human relations. Sin is a condition or state rather than mere act, in which the whole social fabric is infected'. It follows that repentance (*metanoia*) involves not only putting our personal lives to right but also playing a part in the transformation of society. The disciple's faith is that the kingdom or rule of God is inaugurated in Christ, and we are called to work toward its completion.

The kingdom will not be completed until the *eschaton*, the end-time, when 'Christ will come again' and 'God will be all in all'. But like the mustard seed it can grow, and the followers of Jesus are to tend to its growth. 'The growth of the Kingdom of God takes place in human history through liberation in all its forms', says Julie Clague. 'God's action in history (especially through Christ) has been to bring liberation to the oppressed.'

The relevance of this to the HIV/AIDS pandemic scarcely needs elaboration. 'When applied to the devastating consequences of the HIV/AIDS pandemic a liberation theology approach attempts to incarnate a Gospel response, confident that Jesus, in his life and ministry, was closest not to the morally upright but to those whose lives were in collapse. Liberation theology approaches to HIV analyse the unjust structures that are at play in the spread of the pandemic and turn to the liberating good news of the Gospel to address these sinful causes, to provide care and advocacy and to empower those laid low by its impact.' Clague's essay explores what this might concretely mean.

The choice of readings for this collection was suggested by their proven usefulness in introducing students to the foundations of moral theology, especially for the purposes of group discussion. Each is informative, providing access to a wealth of knowledge, as far as possible in non-technical language, or at any rate careful to explain the technical terms. Each is stimulating and challenging: their authors are themselves engaged with and by the questions which they treat, and they bring to their task their personal experience and conviction as well as professional expertise. It will have been noticed that there is some overlap in the material, and some themes recur. This is inevitable in a work about basics but useful also in showing how the basics are interconnected and interdependent.

All of the readings are previously published: Donal Harrington's *What is Morality?* (Columba Press 1996); Hugh Connolly's *Sin* (Continuum 2002); those of Vincent MacNamara, Bill Cosgrave, Pádraig Hogan and Elizabeth Rees have appeared in *The Furrow;* Linda Hogan's in *Doctrine and Life;* and Julie Clague's on the CAFOD website. I am grateful to the authors, journal editors, publishers and CAFOD for permission to publish the material in this volume.

The volume was conceived as a companion to my own *Moral Decision Making* (Veritas 2005) which itself embodies the content of a course of introductory lectures in moral theology. Each of the readings takes a major theme further, enabling the student to explore some particular topics in more depth.

FIVE WAYS OF LOOKING
AT MORALITY

—— Donal Harrington ——

The main concern of this chapter is to present in outline five different but inter-related ways of looking at morality.

From What to How

People differ in their views on moral issues both in the Church and in society generally today. Such difference may well be the most striking aspect of the contemporary experience of morality, though some would find it confusing while others find it enriching. But underneath the different views people have on particular issues, there are different ideas as to what morality itself is.

These underlying differences are reflected in the language people use. One person says: 'If you do what you feel is right, then you are right.' Another says: 'Young people don't know the Ten Commandments anymore.' Yet another says: 'All that really matters is love.' Such differences themselves raise further questions. Should we do as we feel or as we are told? Is there an objective right and wrong? Is love enough?

For the moment, though, let us stay with the statement that people differ in their ideas as to what morality means. Frequently these ideas are more implicit than explicit. People may be quite clear in their own minds as to their views on the rights and wrongs of lying or violence or divorce or euthanasia. But their differences on such issues may conceal underlying differences about the nature of morality and of which the individuals themselves are not fully aware.

In order to get in touch with these underlying ideas, we would need to stand back a little from the firmness of our convictions and the heat of debate. We would need to turn the spotlight from what we think to *how* we think. We might then find that there is a range of factors that come into play in moral discussions, such as feeling and principles and love and consequences. We might find that our own personal style or method of thinking represents a good balance of these factors, or that it emphasises some more than others, or even that it concentrates on one to the neglect of others.

Some may have already worked out these matters for themselves. Many of us, however, will not have done so. Many of us have simply fallen into a particular way of thinking. That style of thinking may have come from our parents or it may have come from reacting against our parents. It may have come from the culture or it may be counter-cultural. But the point is that it is more like something that has happened to us than something we have really sorted out for ourselves. As a result we may be less free than we suppose in our ethical thinking.

The concern of this chapter is to make explicit some of these underlying ways of thinking about morality. We will identify and outline five different ways of thinking about morality. These are:

1 Morality understood as law;
2 Morality as inner conviction;
3 Morality as personal growth;
4 Morality as love;
5 Morality as social transformation.

It may well be that the reader will think of other approaches, or will prefer to put these ones differently, but these five seem to be fairly representative of the range of ways we see morality. While it will be easy to recognise all five, we may be able to recognise only some of them in a way we ourselves think. All five are right in the sense that each stands for some important aspect of morality. One might, however, feel that some present a fuller picture than others.

Somebody once used the phrase: 'the truth looks different from here.' The phrase suggests both a sense that there is something objective and a sense that there are different perspectives. There is something that we call morality, but it looks different from different perspectives. It is like looking into a room through its different windows; each view is real and true and still it is only one view. Somewhat similarly, each of these five ways of looking at morality is a valid view, but only the five together yield a complete picture.

Morality as Law

The first way of looking at morality is to see it in terms of law. This is probably the one that will be most familiar to us, both from our experience of living in society and from our experience in the Church. But it is also one that is often dismissed too hastily because of the negative connotations it can have.

In this view morality is something external, in the sense that it is not something of our own creation but rather something that imposes itself on us. It is given to us, not made by us; something we discover and not something we create. One thinks of the famous line in Sophocles' play *Antigone* where the eponymous heroine resists the unjust laws of King Creon.

> Nor did I think that your orders were so strong
> that you, a mortal man, could over-run the gods'
> unwritten and unfailing laws.

To speak of morality as law is to speak of it as being bigger than any of us. While society can make and change its laws, the moral law is different. It is beyond our determination and to it we must submit.

Because morality is understood as coming from outside of us, it is often associated with an authority figure. Morality is seen to come from our parents, or the parish priest, or the Pope. If this aspect is strongly emphasised, it can appear that a particular action is wrong or right because this figure says so, rather than on the grounds of rational arguments. Some people who see morality this way, when asked why a particular action is wrong, cannot give any reasons other than 'because the Pope (or some other authority figure) says so'.

The truth, however, is that not alone does morality come from outside of us, but it also comes outside such authority figures. In other words, morality is founded on the nature of things and not on any individual will; it is objective. What morality understood as law emphasises is that there is a moral order to the universe and that it is not within any human being's power to decide what that order is. At the same time we can work it out, through reflection and discussion. To help us work it out, authority figures interpret this order to us or for us; but they do not create it.

Because this view of morality is so closely associated in our minds with authority, our own role has often been cast in terms of duty or obedience. It is probably no exaggeration to say that, a generation or two ago, such words seemed to sum up what for most people morality was all about. Obedience was the fundamental virtue. One thinks of the words of Jesus: 'Do you thank the servant because he did what was commanded? So you also, when you have done all that was commanded of you, say "We are unworthy servants; we have only done what was our duty"' (Lk 17:9-10).

We could easily slip into caricature when reflecting on the language of authority and obedience in morals, and so these words of Jesus are salutary. Of course, obedience may and often does become blind but in the present context what the word entails primarily is the recognition that the moral order is something greater than ourselves, not of our own making, and therefore demanding our profound respect.

The words *reward* and *punishment* are also very much a part of this way of looking at morality. They stand for the outcomes of moral behaviour. If morality comes to me as a demand from without, as law, and if the response called for is a sense of duty and an attitude of obedience, then reward is what follows on such a response, punishment on its opposite. The sanctions themselves may be anything from a sweet or a spanking for a child, to the eternal sanctions we know as heaven and hell.

Sometimes it is felt that this language betrays a selfish moral attitude. The morality of Christians is compared with that of others who have no religious affiliation. It is said that, for the latter, morality is purer because it is done for its own sake, whereas the religious motivation may be far from other-centred and more a matter of 'saving my soul'. No doubt this is sometimes the case and it is another instance of how the view of morality as law may become distorted.

Morality as Inner Conviction

The term 'inner conviction' not alone describes the second way of looking at morality, but also captures the contrast between it and the first way. Whereas in the first way morality came from without, here it arises from within. This too can be caricatured, as if morality were simply something we make up for ourselves as we go along. Rather, what is meant is that morality has been internalised. It is not simply an imposition by some authority, demanding our obedience, but it is a requirement arising from an inner conviction.

As a psychological experience, inner conviction comes later in life than obedience. A child can obey without knowing why; it is only later that we grow in the capacity to think for ourselves. But when we can think out right and wrong for ourselves, then we make the law our own. Now we can see for ourselves why the law commends this and forbids that. It is now an inner law, where values are personal convictions and not arbitrary impositions. In exceptional cases we may even come to the conviction that a particular formulation of the moral law is wrong or inapplicable or in conflict with moral value.

This inner law goes by the name of conscience and thus conscience is a key word within this second perspective on morality. Vatican II's document *The Church in the Modern World* put it that 'deep within our conscience we discover a law which we have not laid upon ourselves but which we must obey' (paragraph 16). This is the inner law, the law which has become part of a person, a person's own conscientious conviction. We come to the stage, for instance, when we no longer need another to tell us not to steal because we have come to see and feel its injustice for ourselves.

But at this stage, the language of law and obedience, which is used in the quotation from Vatican II, begins to appear inadequate because of its external focus. To describe what is meant by being moral or not being moral, words like *integrity* and *authenticity* are now more appropriate. If values are internalised and if conviction comes from within, then morality is a matter of being faithful to our inner voice or inner wisdom. This is what is meant by speaking of a person of integrity, one who does not betray deeply held convictions on what is felt to be right because of some temptation of gain or some pressure of the moment.

Likewise, the language of reward and punishment – as when it is said that God rewards the good and punishes the wicked – yields to something less extrinsic. If morality comes from within it hardly makes sense to think in terms of an external authority conferring reward or punishment. Instead, reward and punishment are seen as self-bestowed or self-inflicted. This is where we speak of the alternatives of inner peace *versus* inner disquiet.

The inner peace of a good conscience attends the knowledge that I have been true to my principles. The reward is all the greater if this integrity has been achieved at some price, if it has cost some sacrifice along the way. On the other hand, an inner disquiet accompanies the realisation that I have failed myself by going against what I know to be right. I feel guilty, my conscience is pained. To the conscientious person, no externally imposed punishment could be more painful than this disappointment with self.

Morality as Personal Growth
With this third way of looking at morality we achieve a very valuable expansion of our understanding. What sets it off from the first two ways is that, whereas they focus mainly on our moral behaviour in itself, what we do and what we shun, now the focus is shifted onto ourselves. We move, in other words, from the action being done to the person doing it. Our attention shifts to what is happening the person as a result of the action.

Take, for example, the telling of lies. We can speak in terms of a commandment that prohibits telling lies, and we can even inquire what exceptions there might be to this command. In terms of morality as inner conviction, we can speak of a conscientious conviction as to the wrongfulness of deceit and the harmfulness of deceiving. But this third view of morality adds a further perspective by asking: what happens the person? It suggests that the real tragedy in deceit lies not in the infringement of a law but in a person's becoming dishonest, or in a relationship becoming false thereby.

In the moral tradition this way of seeing things is represented by the language of *virtue* and *vice*. While this language has lost much of its richness today (think of phrases such as a person of 'easy virtue' or 'the vice squad'), within the moral tradition it refers to a way of thinking about morality that emphasises the personal qualities that are the outcome of behaving consistently in determinate ways. Virtues and vices are the good and bad dispositions or qualities that result from and the inspire our actions.

If I repeatedly lie, I become more of a deceitful person, and the more I do so, the more am I inclined by this vicious quality to behave thus on future occasions. And the same is true of the converse. Thomas Aquinas remarked that it is very hard for people in the state of grace to commit sin, because their whole inclination goes against it. Thus virtues and vices might be called moral habits. They are dispositions which arise out of patterns of behaviour and which then dispose the person to act in certain ways in the future.

It is worth noting that this way of thinking is of great antiquity, just as is the language of law. While the Old Testament was setting forth what we know as the Ten Commandments, the Greek philosophers Plato and Aristotle were articulating a view of morality in terms of virtue. Their influence is reflected in the fact that the great thirteenth-century theologian Thomas Aquinas, in composing the moral section of his compendium of theology, the *Summa Theologiae*,

chose virtue rather than commandment as his framework –
the theological virtues of faith, hope and charity and the
cardinal virtues of prudence, justice, courage and temperance.
It is only in more recent centuries that the language of law has
dominated to the extent of almost eclipsing from our horizon
the language of virtue.

In shifting the focus back to what is happening the person,
we also move from a more static to a more dynamic view of
morality. The first and second views tend to be concerned in
their different ways with the rights and wrongs of particular
actions. But if the focus is on what is happening the person,
then that allows us to speak of change in the person, be it
development or regression. This is the language of moral
conversion. It gives us access to the dynamics of challenge and
change, of what it is like for people to try to change for the
better.

Finally there are the outcomes of morality as understood
within this view. Previously we had spoken of reward and
punishment and of good or uneasy conscience. In this third
view we would speak of the contrast of wholeness *versus*
fragmentation. The personal qualities that we call virtues are
many, such as truthfulness, courage, humility, non-violence,
compassion. Each might be seen as a partial realisation of self.
So growth in virtue is a many-sided challenge and as growth
proceeds on different fronts, albeit unevenly, we are becoming
whole, the fully-rounded persons that God envisaged in our
creation. Conversely, when virtue is mingled with vice, to that
extent the thrust towards wholeness is frustrated and our moral
being is becoming fragmented.

Morality as Love
For all that we have referred to already, there are still vast areas
of morality that we have not touched on. This is because the
first three perspectives all concentrate on the moral agent as an

individual person. The remaining two perspectives add to this considerably by seeing morality in terms of relationship and by seeing the moral agent as fundamentally social. This, of course, is a welcome corrective to individualistic tendencies in moral thinking.

In speaking of morality as love, we have in mind the idea that we are primarily relational beings. To explain this we might think of the analogy of the pieces in a chess game. Apart from their place on the board the pieces are incomprehensible, shorn of their essential meaning. Likewise, people are social. They exist in relation to one another as do the pieces on the board. Apart from the other we are cut off from essential aspects of what we are. Even hermits have spoken of their 'leaving' the world as a way of coming closer to the world.

Contemporary philosophy highlights the category of 'the other'. This suggests that the primary moral experience is an experience of other persons. Or, to use an image popular in moral theology, the structure of moral reality is one of 'invitation and response'. Because we inhabit the same space, each of us, simply by virtue of our common humanity, exerts a call or invitation to each other. My presence before you is implicitly a call on you for your kindness and courtesy, a call on your sense of fairness and your sense of sympathy.

Within this perspective, being moral is a matter of being faithful to the fact of our interrelatedness and to the demands of relationship. It is about becoming alive to the fact, and being responsive to the demands that it entails. It is about going beyond ourselves, transcending our own egoism and egoistic horizons, and in the process realising our existence as love – realising that what we are and can be is simply 'love'.

The alternative to this is betrayal. Betrayal means any stance or act or omission that amounts to a denial of our common humanity. Because morality is cast in terms of interrelatedness, what wrong-doing amounts to is basically a matter of betrayal of others or another, rather than a private matter. However, it should also be said that in failing others we are also failing ourselves. In not responding to the demands of a relationship we are also betraying ourselves and missing out on our own self-realisation.

When morality is seen as love, the outcomes of being moral might be expressed in terms of communion *versus* isolation. Whereas reward and punishment refer to what happens people as a consequence of their actions, these terms speak of what happens to a relationship. Insofar as people assent to the invitation–response structure of existence, they grow in communion; insofar as they do not respond to the demands of relationship, they betray, and the outcome is isolation.

The words *communion* and *isolation* give a deeper insight into the meaning of reward and punishment. If morality is about responding in relationship, then communion is clearly the 'reward', though reward is no longer a serviceable term, as it suggests something extrinsically added, whereas communion is the intrinsic outcome of being faithful to each other. Likewise, isolation is punishment in this intrinsic sense rather than an externally imposed sanction. When we recall that without relationship there is no flourishing, we can appreciate how great a punishment it is.

Morality as Social Transformation

The fifth and final way of looking at morality opens on to yet a further horizon. It continues to see morality as a relationship but it goes beyond the small world of interpersonal relationships to the larger world that is society. And just as the view of morality as love was seen as a corrective to individualism in morality, so this broader view is to be welcomed for transcending the tendency to live within our own small circle without any great advertence to the moral issues affecting society or the world as a whole. It also transcends the tendency to tribalism, the attitude that sees moral obligation extending only to our own – the attitude Jesus had in mind when he said: 'For if you love those who love you, what reward do you have? Do not even the tax collectors do the same?' (Mt 5:46).

So moral obligation, like the ripples in the water, keeps reaching outwards. There is nobody who is not our neighbour; all humanity in some real way calls for our response. The word that stands for this perspective is 'justice' – a word that has come dramatically to the centre of moral consciousness in contemporary society. This is not to say that justice had hitherto been neglected; rather it has emerged with new meaning.

The classical definition was that justice is the constant determination to give to every person what is due to that person. However, it is fair to say that we have tended to think about this largely with reference to one-to-one relationships. What is new about today's sense of justice is its sense of responsibility, not just to the individual other, but also for the 'whole state of affairs'. This is captured by the now widely used term 'social justice'.

In this fifth way of looking at morality, being moral is about being personally affected by suffering and injustice and being motivated to do what one can in response. It is about a sense of solidarity with victims, all who lose out or are discriminated against or suffer, be they as near as next door or far across the globe. And responding is not just a matter of providing immediate aid; it also involves asking why the wrongs are happening and questioning the way things are structured in society.

The opposite of such solidarity is individualism. The pressure of competition encourages the individualistic mentality that it is everyone for himself or herself. When this mentality pervades, justice is reduced to keeping within the law, and any sense of solidarity is numbed by the pressure to get on and to succeed. It is not that getting on and succeeding are anything but good, but that something serious is wrong when their pressure is such as to numb the sense of solidarity, or even to rationalise it away in phrases such as 'a rising tide lifts all boats' and 'it's their own fault if they're poor'.

The possible outcomes of morality on this view could be described in terms of social peace *versus* division. When there is a lively sense of solidarity there is the possibility of transforming society into a place where the humanity of each is cherished and where nobody's suffering is tolerated. In the Christian tradition this is what is known as peace. To quote again from *The Church in the Modern World* (paragraph 78): 'Peace is more than the absence of war ... A firm determination to respect the dignity of other persons and other peoples, along with the deliberate practice of fraternal love, are absolutely necessary for the achievement of peace.' Whereas if the individualistic ethic prevails, to that extent the divisions that are already there are only deepened and, as the saying goes, the rich get richer and the poor get poorer.

Finally, a further dimension of this view of morality should be acknowledged. It is that, as the concept of justice has broadened in recent times in the way described, it has also come to embrace the issue of humanity's relationship to the environment and to proclaim this to be a moral question of immense proportions. In some real sense, our 'solidarity' is to be with all of creation. We are to understand all creation as one great community or partnership of being and we, the conscious or reflective level in the whole of creation, are called to learn respect and to repent abuse.

Morality as Law
Duty, Obedience   Reward versus Punishment

Morality as Inner Conviction
Conscience, Integrity   Inner Peace versus Disquiet

Morality as Personal Growth
Virtue, Conversion   Wholeness versus Fragmentation

Morality as Love
Faithfulness, Response   Communication versus Isolation

Morality as Social Transformation
Justice, Solidarity   Social Peace versus Division

Integrating the Five Approaches

As we said at the start, we have each of us our own way of seeing morality and this five-fold schematisation may help to make explicit for each of us the way we have been seeing things. But if it transpires that one of these ways has taken precedence in our thinking, the question arises as to how we can take account of, and incorporate, the other four.

For a start it might be remarked that the five are not so self-contained as to have no relationship to each other. There are certain points of contact and we could even regard each of the five as seeing the same truth through a different 'window', so that we can translate from one to another. For example, where the law says 'thou shalt not kill', the language of personal growth would speak of the call to become a non-violent person. Again, it is not so much that 'inner peace' and 'communion', or 'duty' and 'integrity', are different realities, as that they are different ways of talking about a single reality.

So we can say that all five perspectives are right. Each offers some indispensable truth about and insight into morality, yet each on its own is incomplete. Each possesses a piece of the truth so that, on its own, it is both valuable and partial. Even as we moved from one to the next, we saw new horizons on morality opening up, challenging us to achieve a comprehensive viewpoint. Each of us is still entitled to our preference, in the sense of being attracted to either law or inner conviction or personal growth or love or social transformation as the motif of our moral sensibility. But we are also obliged to take account of the other four and to integrate them into our perspective.

Failure to integrate one with the rest leaves us with an impoverished and possibly distorted perspective. This failure accounts for many aberrations in moral theory and practice. For instance, what is 'legalism' but a focus on the first approach which neglects the other four? Surely moral law is an articulation of what justice in society is all about, of what love means, of the direction in which personal growth is to be pursued, of how inner conviction is to be formed. If our appreciation of moral law is not informed and inspired by these further perspectives, then it becomes just law absorbed in itself, missing the wood for the trees – so that people are burdened with demands that make no sense because there is no meaningful reference frame.

Likewise, what is 'subjectivism' but an adoption of the second approach that ignores the rest? Inner conviction is a valid base from which to talk about morality, but subjectivism in its perjorative sense means an emphasis on 'following my conscience' that is oblivious to the truth that conscience itself is nothing other than the capacity to appreciate the underlying meaning of moral law, of the dynamics of moral growth, and of the complex demands of love and justice.

If morality as personal growth is taken on its own, it may be reduced to a search for personal fulfilment that has little reference to others. What the moral law reveals is that personal growth is a matter of love and justice, and without this understanding we may be left with a much impoverished idea of growth as pursuit of fulfilment in a very self-centred sense.

In relation to the fourth approach taken on its own, we might refer to the term 'situation ethics'. This stands for the theory which holds that morality has only one absolute, namely, to do the loving thing. After that, it depends on the situation what the loving thing may be. Here love comes to mean nothing because it can mean anything. It lacks any of the definition it would have if it were to be interpreted in the light of the other ways of seeing morality.

Lastly, commitment to justice is distorted if seen in isolation. It must be subject to the demands of love and integrity if it is not to justify the use of any means in achieving its ends. One thinks of the utilitarian theory of 'the greatest good of the greatest number', whereby the individual might be sacrificed for the sake of the greater good. The desirability of what is striven after does not give a *carte blanche* to achieve it by any means.

All the same, such absolutising of a single perspective is understandable. Those who ask where the Ten Commandments have gone may feel that the only way to preserve the sense of right and wrong in society is to keep insisting on the need for law. But others feel equally strongly that we need to celebrate and cherish inner convictions because for too long people have been slave to moral authority, unable to think for themselves, crippled by guilt. Others again say that all this is futile theorising and is taking our attention away from the real issues of injustice and violence in the world.

We can readily see the legitimacy of each concern, but we can also note the blindspot in each. Ultimately the absolutising of any one approach distorts our whole understanding of morality. If each approach could appreciate the insight contained in the other perspectives, a fuller truth would become available.

It is worth applying all this to the 'generation gap' as it affects morality and moral consciousness. The generations formed prior to Vatican II were formed very much along the lines of morality as law, while it is largely the younger generations that toast the language of freedom and conscience. The word 'largely' is used because there are many older people who have experienced the release of escaping from the painful constraints of law-become-legalism.

If we listen to the older generation we often hear, besides genuine admiration for the young, a bemoaning of 'the youth' and their (supposed) loss of moral standards, of their being captives to subjectivism and relativism. There is much truth in this, especially in thinking of it as a captivity. But there is also the shining truth that it is among the young that commitment to the fifth perspective, that of social solidarity and transformation, is most vibrant. Among young people, sexual morality is nowhere as black-and-white as among their parents; but they can be very absolute and unyielding in their moral principles concerning injustice, war and ecological destruction. Seen in this light, morality seen as law is alive and well, just that it has to be looked for somewhere else than hitherto.

The Five Approaches and Christian Morality
Up to this point, reference to God or to religion has been incidental, as we have been concentrating on morality in itself and on the different ways in which it can be understood. But if we now turn our attention to religion and morality, the question arises: does one or other of these perspectives do better justice than the others to the meaning of Christian morality? If each were imagined to be a kind of key, is there

one which unlocks more of what Christian morality is all about? Or if each were seen as a language for speaking about morality, are some better able than others to articulate the full dimensions of Christian morality?

We might begin answering this question by noting that all five can be found represented in the Bible. The language of law is found throughout the Bible, in the Old Testament particularly. Many would think immediately of the Ten Commandments. If morality is approached in terms of inner conviction, we might think of the biblical theme of the 'heart' as the source of moral decisions, or of Jesus' emphasis on the significance of the intention behind the action. When it comes to the language of personal growth, Paul's three great virtues of faith, hope and charity come to mind. Morality as love is familiar through all the pages of the Gospels. And when one thinks of morality as social transformation, the concern of the prophets for right relationships in society, as well as Jesus' love for the poor, come to mind.

All five are there in the pages of scripture, but it is perhaps fair to say that the language of law is the one that has preoccupied us. The tendency has been to view biblical morality through the lens of law. However, this is not so much because law is the dominant biblical perspective, as that it is what has dominated our approach to the Bible. And even though the language of law figures very prominently throughout the Bible, it can be argued both that it is not the crucial perspective in the Bible and that, as a key, it is limited in what it can unlock of the riches of biblical and Christian morality.

Indeed, if we confine ourselves to this approach we will quickly run into paradox. There is the paradox that to love simply in obedience to a commandment is not really to love. There is the paradox that Christians must be obedient as 'slaves of Christ' even though the same Christ has set them free (Gal 5). Such paradoxes do not make the language of law invalid; they just reveal its limitations.

When Paul speaks of 'the law of the Spirit of life in Christ Jesus' (Rom 8:2), and when Thomas Aquinas speaks of the 'New Law' which is 'chiefly the grace itself of the Holy Spirit' (*Summa Theologiae*, II-I, 106, 1), it is clear that the idea of law cannot contain what they are talking about unless its meaning be transformed. They indicate to us that the language of law is inadequate for unlocking the deep meaning of Christian morality.

We might go on to suggest that the language of the second and third ways of looking at morality are incomplete also. For one thing, they are too much focused on the individual, whereas the Bible is more properly focused on the salvation of a people. They also concentrate on what the person is doing, whereas the Bible concentrates on the action of God as primary.

All this leads us to the fourth and fifth perspectives, with their language of invitation-response and of social transformation. These are perhaps the most promising approaches to the Bible. The covenant that lies at the heart of both testaments is presented as God's invitation calling on our response. And responding as a people to God's invitation is seen as the way towards right relationships throughout society.

Five Approaches: Three Styles

The final concern of this chapter will be to comment on the five approaches as they have manifested themselves in recent history of moral theology. We would suggest that, when viewed in this historical context, they can be distilled down to three groups, representing what might be called on 'objective', a 'subjective' and a 'social' style of moral reflection, and that these appear as successive emphases in the recent history.

Objective	— >	Morality as Law
	>	Morality as Inner Conviction
Subjective	— >	Morality as Personal Growth
	>	Morality as Love
Social	— >	Morality as Social Transformation

The style of moral theology up to the middle of the twentieth century was very objective, very much a morality in terms of law. By objective is meant an approach to morality that concentrates on the action that is done or omitted. It works out whether a given line of action is right or wrong and it does this by considering, not so much the consequences of the act, but the principles and values that should guide moral behaviour, and the conformity, or lack of it, of the particular action to such principles or values.

This style allows for the consideration of possible exceptions to the rule and the justification, if any, for such exceptions. It also includes consideration of factors such as fear or ignorance, which may diminish the person's freedom and responsibility. But what is notable is the brevity of the discussion of such factors, no more than a few pages in most texts, which effectively constituted no more than a footnote. (What this means is that the more subjective aspects of morality lose out in the concentration on the objective.)

In the years leading up to Vatican II, there emerged a new emphasis on morality from a subjective or personalist perspective, that is, with the focus on the person acting and not just on the act being done. Originally this was inspired by the renewed scriptural scholarship of the previous decades. That scholarship brought out the centrality in the Bible of themes such as conversion, discipleship and love. While at the heart of the Gospels, these were strangely subdued and often absent in moral theology; in effect moral theology was often no more than moral philosophy. Books appeared in the 1950s with titles such as *The Primacy of Charity in the Moral Life, The Master Calls* and, best known, Bernard Häring's *The Law of Christ*. Häring's foreword announced that moral theology was to be focused on Christ and that it could not be viewed solely from the point of view of law.

The word *personalist* well describes this enrichment to moral theology. Without any depreciation of objectivity in morals, it brings the person to centre stage. It considers morality as a personal calling; it reflects on what that calling is and on what it entails. We can readily see how the perspectives on morality as inner conviction and as personal growth correspond with this. Seeing morality as love also belongs here, in that the personal calling that is at the heart of Christian morality is fundamentally a call to love.

● In more recent years there has been taking place a further development in moral theology, which might be described as a move from the personal to the social. Of course, to see morality as love is already to see it as social, but this is social only in a modified sense. This is because, despite the personalist enrichment of a hitherto objectivist moral theology, much of the thrust was still in terms of an individual person making a moral decision and on the demands of interpersonal relationships. Much of the focus has now shifted from the decision and action to the person deciding, but the frame was still largely individualist.

The shift to the social in moral theology has to do with its experiencing the fruits of the 'liberation theology' that swept into western thinking from Latin America in the 1970s. Here, theology starts with reflecting on the inequalities and injustices in society. This contrasts with the previous style, which discussed mainly the rights and wrongs of an individual's actions. It corresponds to the shift that begins in our fourth way of looking at morality (morality as love) and which emerges fully in the perspective that sees morality in terms of justice and social transformation.

With this scheme of objective-personalist-social in mind, we can ask how different people in the Church think about morality today. We can ask: how do members of Christ's faithful actually think about and think through their Christian morality? How do moral theologians think about morality? How do Church leaders think about morality?

Take moral theologians first. It is quite surprising how many textbooks presenting themselves as introductions to moral theology, many of them regarded as 'state of the art' works, contain little or no reference to the themes of justice and social transformation. These are left to 'applied' moral theology. In their methodology moral theologians are still very much involved in the transition from an objective to a personalist way of seeing morality. This may explain why themes such as freedom, conscience and authority are such major preoccupations in their writings.

If the discipline of moral theology is still thus engaged in the debate on the relationship between objective and subjective morality, Church teaching about morality appears even less attentive to subjective or personalist aspects. This would seem to be because of its concern to protect an object moral order against the perceived threat of relativism. However, it must be said that many Church documents are much more alive to morality in the socio-political mode, as is witnessed by a now century-long tradition of social teaching.

What then of the individual disciple? How does he or she think about morality? There is hardly a single answer. Some think very much in the language of conscience and feel great tension in relation to the morality of law and authority. Others are firmly rooted in the language of law. Others again find themselves uncomfortably between the two. Others still have been taken up by the cries for justice in the world and see morality very much through the prism of this passion. At the end of this chapter the question that is left for each of us is: where do you stand yourself?

IS THERE A
NATURAL LAW?

— Donal Harrington —

Our reflections on the approach to morality as law have shown that this is an essential perspective on morality. In this chapter we seek to deepen our appreciation of this perspective by reflecting on the theme of the natural law. This is the theme that reveals what it means most fundamentally to see morality as law.

Natural Law Today

A brief note about terminology may be helpful, as the term 'natural law' is itself confusing. At first sight the term might suggest the laws of nature such as are formulated in the natural sciences. It is, for instance, a law of nature that mass can be converted into energy, or that moths are attracted to light, or that daffodils bloom in the springtime. These are laws about what is the case in nature. They define inevitabilities or probabilities that are built into how things are.

In morality, natural law refers to human beings specifically; it is more accurately spoken of as natural moral law. Here 'law' is not a description of what is, but a formulation of what should be. It is a normative rather than a descriptive term. To speak of the natural moral law is to say that the basis for moral law, for what people should do and what they should avoid, is to be found in our nature as human beings. This means that what we are, our nature, contains indications as to how we should live. There is no such 'should' at any other level of created being.

Frequently when the idea of law is used in moral discourse, it is understood as something that somebody decides, rather like the way legislators might determine laws on divorce or drink-driving or the prevention of terrorism. Such laws might be otherwise, and are indeed different in other countries, but they are what they are because this is what has been decided. But the natural moral law is not the outcome of human determination. It is a law in the sense of something inbuilt and prior to our decisions, something we discover rather than something we determine.

For all its prominence within the Catholic moral tradition, there are a number of difficulties with the natural law theory. Firstly, there exist different versions of what natural law means, and we shall refer to a couple of these below. Obviously, it makes critical discussions of the idea of natural law very frustrating if it is not clear what people are actually talking about or if they are talking about different ideas.

Secondly, in an age when change is so much our experience of history, the idea of natural law can sound quite frozen. We have almost got used to rapid and accelerating change as part of human life. This change brings with it previously unimaginable ethical dilemmas, but it also throws up new perceptions on the meaning and possibilities of human existence. For many, this conflicts with the idea of a natural law formulated for once and for all, reflecting a permanent and unchanging human reality.

Thirdly, it can be hard to reconcile the idea of a natural law with the fact of cultural variation. The diversity across different cultures concerning the moral rights and wrongs of issues, ranging from polygamy to cannibalism, renders it difficult to argue that all humanity shares a common morality. One is tempted to conclude that morality is culturally determined rather than universally prescribed and that there is in fact no such thing as a universal moral truth. This would reduce what is moral to what is conventional.

This relates to a scepticism today about the very possibility of moral truth. To say, for instance, that contraception frustrates the proper functioning and true purpose of human sexuality, or that the needs of the poor are prior to the right to private property, can seem to be no more than one group's version of what the moral truth is. It might well be that others agree broadly on what it is to be a human being, and yet are puzzled or unconvinced by, or vehemently disagree with, such conclusions. They do not see why what we are necessarily implies that this is how we are to behave. They suggest that directives for living cannot be read off so simply.

As against such difficulties, there remains the suspicion that without some kind of natural law there may be no morality at all. It is hard to imagine, for instances, how we can come to terms with the ecological crisis or with the challenge to international peace without some universal ethic and universally applicable values. If, with the transformation of communications, we live in a 'global village' then we would expect that there would be some global ethic to guide our life together. Despite all the pluralism that exists in morals, the way the world is going seems to demand some basic morality in common for all humanity.

But even apart from that, it makes sense to think that if there is a common human nature then there would also be some common human morality, however general or specific it might be. And if there is no universal basis for moral discourse, it does not seem to make sense to speak of a human nature that is shared by all of humanity, and whereby we are all moral beings.

A Way of Thinking

There are two ways of approaching the idea of natural law. It can be seen as a theory which tells us what is right and wrong, or it can be seen as a theory which tells us how to go about finding out what is right and wrong. It is probably more helpful to start with the latter, as it is the more fundamental.

Natural law is basically a way of going about the business of ascertaining right and wrong. It says that we come to moral truth by using our reason to reflect upon our human nature. Natural law is this method of reason reflecting on nature, through which we discover moral truth. Here the word 'reason' is not meant to sound excessively rationalistic. In moral reflection it is good to think in terms of 'the reasoning heart', that is, of a form of reflection that integrates thought and affectivity. Again, the word 'nature' is not meant to thingify personhood. Reason reflecting on nature means people reflecting on their own human being and their own experience of being human. It means reflecting on what it is to be a human person.

This method stands out more sharply if we contrast it with other ways of finding out what is right and wrong. There are two in particular which are prominent in contemporary moral consciousness. One is sometimes called subjectivism or emotivism. It sees moral statements (statements that such-and-such an action is right or wrong) to be no more than statements of subjective preference. Here, deciding what to do depends on consulting our feelings and convictions. If two people then disagree, for instance, about the morality of euthanasia, it is essentially no different from their disagreeing about the merits of Indian food. There is no accounting for taste, and there is no accounting for moral viewpoints. In other words, there is no further court of appeal.

Where this method sees moral truth as no more than the truth of what one feels, another method for determining right and wrong finds moral truth by weighing up the consequences of different courses of action. It is sometimes called consequentialism or utilitarianism. The action that offers the best outcomes for all concerned is the one with the greatest utility value, and is therefore judged to be right. The outcomes in question are sometimes defined by the phrase, 'the greatest happiness of the greatest number'.

Now it is eminently sensible, when deciding what to do, both to consult our feelings and to consider the consequences of possible courses of action. So we do not wish to suggest that a choice has to be made for one of these methods and against the other. Indeed, the ideal might well be an integration of the different methods. That is to say, when deciding what to do in a given situation, we would have regard both for our own feelings and convictions, and for the likely consequences of the various choices available, as well as for the significance of the choices in relation to the meaning of human existence.

But the natural law method would see the last of these as more fundamental. That does not mean that every decision has to be preceded by an explicit and prolonged reflection on what it is to be a human being; that would be paralysing. More often than not, all that we are doing in the concrete is consulting feelings and weighing up consequences. But there is an underlying stream in our thinking, less often explicit but none the less real, that has to do with how we understand the meaning of being a human person in the world. Though it may be more implicit than explicit, it is the most decisive ingredient in our moral decisions.

Thus, when people disagree about right and wrong, it may be a conflict of feelings or convictions that leads to their difference. Or their disagreement may represent different estimations of the consequences of the various options. But it may also be due to a difference in perceptions of what being a human person is all about. For instance, if people disagree about the rights and wrongs of sex outside marriage, they will argue in vain about what harm sex outside marriage might or might not do, if their real difference is about the significance of sexuality within personal and interpersonal existence.

When we reflect on what it is to be a human person, we may in fact conclude that some of our feelings or convictions are misguided, or that certain consequences we thought desirable are outweighed by other considerations. For instance, we might feel very strongly like executing the perpetrator of a brutal killing, or we might be very tempted by the potential outcome of torturing a terrorist in order to elicit where the bomb has been planted. Natural law would simply advocate that we reflect on what the nature and purpose of human existence might have to say about such courses of action. Otherwise we may find that we have done something that we regard in retrospect to have contradicted what we are. We may torture the terrorist only to find ourselves asking: what does it mean for us as a society, now that we have introduced torture?

To tease this out further, let us take the issue of terminating the life of somebody who is terminally ill. Some family members may want to end the agony of their loved one, while others may regard it as wrong to take life. Feelings and convictions are divided, and no doubt each point of view would argue that its line of action would produce the most desirable outcome. There is a need to look at underlying and perhaps quite unreflected views about the meaning of life and death. Is life to be preserved at any price? Is death a good or an evil? Is there anything after death? Does suffering have any meaning or value?

It is quite possible that all those concerned could discuss all these questions and end up agreeing about the broad meaning of life, death and suffering, yet continue to disagree about what to do in the situation. This tells us that general reflections on the meaning of the human reality do not translate simply into deductions about what to do. But the reflection is vital for a different reason. Without it, how are we to know what is a good consequence as opposed to a bad one? Without it, how are we to know what to feel strongly about? Without it, the convictions we feel and the consequences we seek lack a rational basis.

In other words, there is a basis for moral thinking to be found in reflection on what it means to be a human person. This reflection may not tell us concretely what to do, but it provides directions for thinking. It orients our feelings and forms our convictions in certain directions. It leads us to seek and to value certain kinds of consequences over towers. It means that we will tend to feel strongly about what is conducive to human self-realisation. It means that we will look for options for action that has the consequence of achieving the purposes of our existence.

Room for Creativity

Often there is a suspicion about natural law, that if we base our ethical reflections on the nature of the human person we will end up with a very rigid kind of moral thinking. For this reason it is important to note the balance contained in the definition of natural law as reason reflecting on nature. If we neglect to consider our 'nature', then we will be reasoning without any reference frame or foundation, and our conclusions may be quite arbitrary. But if the element of 'reason' is neglected, the natural law can appear not to require any reflection at all, but only the application to particular situations of directives that have already been worked out elsewhere and which are quite fixed and unyielding.

That this latter has often been the case is the reason for much dissatisfaction with natural law theory. Take for instance the issue of lying. According to a version of natural law which fails to appreciate the role of reason, the purpose of the faculty of speech is clearly that of communicating to others the contents of our mind. While there will be occasions when this would not be appropriate, so that we might withhold the truth, to communicate something contrary to what we know in our minds to be the case would be a misuse and abuse of this faculty and therefore morally wrong.

The reason why this version leaves so little room for human reasoning is that human nature is understood in this case as no more than a physical functioning of the faculty of speech. If, instead of this, we were to think of the natural moral law for humans as a matter of communicating in ways that are faithful to the demands of relationship and the building of communion, we would have a very different picture. The values of fidelity and communion would give us a far stronger and deeper motivation for being truthful. But we could also imagine situations where saying what is not true might actually be the most faithful and truthful thing to do. In discerning when and how that might be so, there would be great demands made on the creativity and imagination of the reasoning heart.

Thus, to say that natural law begins with reason reflecting on nature does not mean that everything is already written into our human nature, simply to be read off. That would correspond to the first version above and it would reduce human nature to something like a computer programme, where all the instructions are written in beforehand. In such a case there would be no room for creativity, but only for applying formulae or deducing from what is already fixed.

The complexity of human nature and of the human reality is of a different order. It is not the complexity of a computer's extraordinarily intricate, but nevertheless pre-written, set of instructions. It is, rather, the complexity of a being which finds itself in this world as a certain kind of being and yet has to find out what kind of being it should be.

The complexity might be expressed by saying that, as reason reflects on the human reality, it discovers that the human being is both pre-determined and undetermined. This introduces the theme of freedom, and touches on the debate between those who say that human beings are radically free and those who argue that we are fundamentally determined, whether by our environment or by our genes or by our unconscious. Without entering into that debate, we wish to suggest that human reality is a combination of both the determined and the undetermined.

A comparison with the animal world clarifies this. Animals are pre-programmed to a great extent, with ranges of agilities and reactions that unfold relatively automatically. Animals blindly follow the instincts and tendencies of their nature. But people are different. Whatever other troubles they might have, dogs do not have to agonise over the meaning of their dogginess. But the experiences that people have in life confront them with questions as to who they are and what it all means. They have to think about what they could be and what they should do. Unlike animals, people will not realise themselves by blindly following their instincts, but only by reflecting on their experience and discovering the imperatives of their nature.

As we reflect, we will discover that in some senses our human nature is something pre-given. In particular, we will discover that there are certain fundamental possibilities that define human existence. These possibilities might be expressed, for example, in the language of virtue. We might speak of virtues such as integrity, love and justice as representing what is both highest and most distinctive about human nature. This much is given, pre-determined; at this level we do not decide about ourselves but rather discover what we are.

But as we reflect, we will also discover that what is given is primarily a task, the task of becoming such a person. It will not happen automatically. Rather, we are free in a very deep sense. We may assent to or reject what we discover to be the deepest possibilities of our nature. As well as that, the times we live in may modify our understanding and appreciation of what it is to be a human being. And then, having gained some insight into what we are to become, there is the task of figuring out what ways of living and relating and behaving will best promote this becoming.

Thus, at the human level, creation is not governed by necessity; there is room for manoeuvre. We find out for ourselves that we have to decide for ourselves what to make of ourselves. We each have to carve out our own personhood from what we are given. We might think of the analogy of a sculptor working on a block of stone, needing both to respect the raw material and to creatively imagine what it might become. We too must shape what we are given; so much so that it can be frightening at times and we would sometimes prefer to have it as easy as the animals.

The Law of our Being

The fact remains that, even if we base our morality in reflecting on the nature of human reality, people still differ about what it is to be a human person. One school of thought will say that, when we reflect on what we are, what we find is simply the inclination to seek pleasure and avoid pain. In contrast to this, traditional natural law theory speaks of the inclinations to preserve life, to procreate and educate offspring, to seek the truth and to cooperate in society. Another philosophy will hold that we find nothing pre-given, but that our human nature is nothing more than what we create through the exercise of our freedom.

But is there anything more fundamental that underlies such various interpretations? One promising approach would be to say that common to all such interpretations is the human spirit in search of moral truth. Natural law is about reflecting on human nature; but if reflection and deliberation are what is distinctively human, then natural law means most fundamentally our reflecting on our own reflecting. Whether our conclusions converge or diverge, we all seek and question according to the same pattern. If so, this pattern is itself the most basic natural moral law. Let us elaborate on this.

At the heart of our moral consciousness there is questioning. First of all, our human experience of good and bad, right and wrong, raises questions of our understanding. As we seek to understand our experience, we come up with different ideas and insights, so that there arise questions for our judgment, which search to see if our understanding is true. This in turn raises questions for deliberation. These questions bring us beyond knowing and feeling to the moment of decision and commitment.

This is the pattern of how we operate as morally conscious subjects, a pattern of experiencing, then understanding, then judging, then deciding. We can say that the pattern is invariant in that, if another were to disagree with the outcomes of our reflections and deliberations, that person would do so by coming to different understandings, judgments, decisions, commitments. Whatever the outcome, the pattern would be the same. Thus we can say that it is our natural orientation to inquire into our experience, to seek insight, to strive to arrive at what is true and what is good, and to commit ourselves to the good that we find.

One can readily see the 'law' that is contained in this pattern and how the pattern can be experienced as a source of obligation. It is the law of being open and attentive to our experience, of being intelligent and insightful in our inquiries, of being reasonable and comprehensive in our judgments, of being detached and responsible in our deliberations, of being committed to the good that we discover. If we observe these 'precepts' well, we will arrive at the true and the good. And this is what the natural law fundamentally is.

In the formulation of Thomas Aquinas seven centuries ago, the basic precept of the natural law is that we should do good and avoid evil. It may sound obvious but what he was stating is that we are moral beings, that we are by nature oriented or inclined towards the good. The above formulation simply develops this by elaborating on the pattern of our moral consciousness. It is this pattern of consciousness that differentiates us from the animals. They do not have to decide about themselves and about what is good. But we do, and this is how we go about it. For this reason, the human person might be described as 'the moral animal'.

From this we can say that the first thing that reason learns from reflecting on human nature concerns the 'how' rather than the 'what' of morality. Our basic learning concerns how to go about being moral beings, namely, by being attentive to our experience, insightful in our thinking, reasonable in our judgments, responsible in our deliberations, committed in our living. This is our nature, our natural inclination as moral beings. What this will tell us about right and wrong is a further question, but this is the path whereby we activate our nature as moral animals.

This much does, however, offer an explanation for at least some of the disagreement that exists about human nature and moral principles. That is to say, people attend, think, reflect, deliberate differently. People attend to different data; they understand differently and come to different conclusions. Some of this is due simply to the enriching fact of diversity. And some of it is the result of ignorance, inadvertence, oversight, blindspots, bias.

Some of the latter in turn has to do with the context, for it does happen that the blindspot or bias may affect a whole community or culture. It may be simply that the individual person has a distorted understanding of, say, property or of sexuality; or it may be that the person is a victim of the distorted understanding of the times he or she lives in. We do not reflect in a vacuum, apart from the culture we live in; on the contrary, that culture significantly modifies our moral sensibility.

This formulation also allows us to affirm a natural law while at the same time taking account of the centrality of change. The world we are in is constantly changing and so too, our perception of ourselves is on the move. But there is a bedrock, namely, our nature as experiencing, inquiring, understanding, knowing, deliberating, loving human beings. This bedrock makes for continuity amidst all the changes in our situation, in our perception of ourselves and in our moral awareness.

A Future Achievement

The focus of our reflections has been on process rather than on content. We have been exploring the fruitfulness of thinking of natural law as the law of how we think about morality rather than as the results of that thinking. An advantage of this approach is that it avoids the impression of natural law as an immovable set of moral directives and emphasises instead the central role of the reasoning heart in the discovery of moral truth.

However, this approach is bound to feel frustrating to those who simply want a statement of what is right and wrong. The basic answer to that sense of frustration is that there is no way of setting forth what is right and wrong that bypasses human minds and hearts. There is no 'objective' formulation of the natural moral law, set in stone for all times and places and requiring nothing more than simple acquiescence on our part.

This is because of the nature of objectivity. In any area of inquiry there is no objectivity without subjectivity. We do not reach the objective truth without successfully negotiating the subjective processes of inquiry, understanding, judgment, decision. But in morality these processes are further complicated by the fact that what we are investigating is ourselves. Some of the phenomenon that scientists seek to understand are outside the scientists themselves. But in moral selection, we ourselves are the phenomenon that we are trying to understand.

There is no formulation of right and wrong that can be advanced so as to end all debate. Reflection on and debate about human experience is the only solution. If we start with people reflecting on what is to be people, if we enter into conversation about our various viewpoints; if in a spirit of dialogue we grow to appreciate what has been called 'the light of disagreement', then we will be progressing towards truth.

For this reason the natural law, in the sense of the outcome of our reflecting and conversing, could be said to lie ahead of us. It is something we strive towards rather than something we possess. In a sense it does not yet exist, because humanity has not yet attained a converging viewpoint as a result of its experiences, insights, judgments and decisions. Put more positively, the natural law exists insofar as people have come to a common perception of and commitment to the truth about themselves. The natural law is future because we as a race are still in the process of discovering who we are and learning to agree on what it means to be a human being.

One modest illustration of this comes from a gathering of people from a variety of world religions in 1993. The gathering styled itself the 'Parliament of the World's Religions' (though those present were not necessarily officially representing their religions), and it produced a declaration on what it called a 'global ethic'. The ethic consists of a 'fundamental demand' and four 'irrevocable directives'. The fundamental demand is that every human being must be treated humanely. The four directives are: commitment to a culture of non-violence and respect for life; commitment to a culture of solidarity and a just economic order; commitment to a culture of tolerance and a life of truthfulness; commitment to a culture of equal rights and partnership between men and women.[1]

To the enlightened this will seem unremarkable, yet something new is happening. People from vastly different cultures are beginning to come together and to agree on fundamental moral values. The values they articulate are very much what the natural law is about, or will be about in the future. These values are what emerge when people join together to attend and inquire, to reason and deliberate, in loving commitment. The results are not so much human constructions as what people discover when they activate their moral consciousness.

One thinks also of the United Nations Human Rights Declaration as a similar process in a secular context. But what it all amounts to is convergence. In one sense the natural law is there already, in the way we are and what we are for. But in another way it lies ahead of us, its unveiling hastened by the convergence of minds and hearts coming together from very varied backgrounds.

This is something that has never happened before in the history of the world. Whenever the natural law was formulated or articulated before, it was from within a single culture, that of Europe. Perhaps that is why the phenomenon of conflicting practices in far-off cultures was so hard to embrace. But now the world is becoming a single unit, a global community. The focus is on dialogue between different perceptions of the moral truth, on different accounts of our moral being coming into conversation. Here, truth is born from the enrichment of diversity.

The outcome of this emerging dialogue is not the kind of standardisation that capitalism is imposing on the world community, nor the kind of moral uniformity that might have characterised single cultures in the past. Rather, the possibility presents itself of diversity being recognised and cherished within a common perception of what it is to be human.

Nevertheless, to think of natural law in this way as a future achievement attendant upon the unity of humankind is far from implying that such an achievement is in any way imminent. Even though there is now a global context for ethical debate, it remains that some of the most intractable difficulties in moral discourse today stem from humanity's inability to agree on fundamental aspects of what it is to be a human being. It is one thing to speak as we have of natural law as being in the future; how short-term or long-term a future is another matter.

All of this echoes points that have always been acknowledged in the Catholic tradition about natural law. That tradition has acknowledged that we do not come to a knowledge of the natural law without difficulty, and that we should not expect that most people would agree on how to understand the natural law. The prospect of hordes of people easily recognising the rights and wrongs of whole ranges of issues, or even agreeing on the underlying principles, is not what natural law means. Confusion and disagreement are much more what is envisaged. The idea of natural law is that there is a moral truth to be found and that we will find it by activating our moral consciousness in communion with one another.

If this is the case, then the clear need is that 'reason' be given the same attention at least as 'nature'. The idea of natural law holds that there is a law of our being that we are called to discover and to cherish. But it does not envisage an easy discovery. The key, then, is that we learn how to reason well with our reasoning hearts, and how to reason well together in a world that, for all its pluralism, is converging into a single community.

The Autonomy of Morality

To speak of natural law is to speak of morality as coming out of who we are. It is to say that we are moral animals and that the kind of being we are is a source of revelation as to how we should live. The question we would now raise is: how does God fit into this way of thinking about morality?

The question is important because we can easily misconceive God's relation to natural law, thereby both discrediting the idea of natural law and distorting our picture of God. In particular, the language of God 'giving' the natural law can be misleading, however valid the intention behind the language. Such language can have the effect that those who do not believe in God are alienated from the idea of a natural moral law.

Much of the misconception comes from the way religion and morality can be bound up together within a given culture. It often happens that people leave the Church because of disagreement over what they obviously regard as significant moral issues. Usually these people still believe in God and are still hungry for spiritual nourishment, and yet departing from the morality and departing from the religion have become almost the same thing. The Christian religion has become identified with its moral teachings, with the resulting tendency in people not to see themselves as part of the religion if they are in disagreement on certain moral issues.

Meanwhile, and the more so the more pluralist society has become, we are confronted with the phenomenon of high morality manifested in people of no religious affiliation or no religious belief. This has led theologians to speak of the 'autonomy' of morality. The fact of morality present in people of no religious conviction suggests that morality can and does exist independently of religion. Just because people give up their religion is no reason for them to give up their morals. Being moral is part of being human, whether a person is religious or not. Some would go so far as to argue that morality is even more fundamentally part of us than is religion.

The alternative to the autonomy of morality is some kind of morality of authority. Rather than morality being part of being human, it is located in an authority figure who 'gives' it to humankind. This could be the crude understanding of what God was doing in giving Moses the Ten Commandments. Or it could be the crude understanding of God 'giving' us the natural law.

In a morality of authority, the rightness or wrongness of a course of action tends to be seen to reside in the will of the authority figure rather than in the nature of things. Why is it wrong to steal? Because it is against the commandments. Why is killing wrong? Because God has told us. Why is abortion wrong? Because the Pope says so. Sometimes this is as far as it goes. But the real questions are only beginning. Why is it against the commandments? Why does God tell us so? Why does the Pope say so? One could even ask flippantly: what if God had a change of mind tomorrow? Would that make something right when today it is wrong? Or are rightness and wrongness inherent in the nature of things (as God has created them)?

The problem with a morality of authority is that it threatens the idea of any universally common morality. If morality is to be found in the will of God, or in the Bible, or in the teachings of the Pope, then what is the situation of one who has not read the Bible, or does not subscribe to the Pope, or does not believe in God? It would seem that such a person has no access to moral truth. For the believer this would mean that God goes on creating millions of human beings who have no way of knowing what God wants from them.

A much more satisfactory view of the matter is to be found in a text we have already quoted from: Paul's letter to the Romans. Some very immoral practices were going on in that community, yet, being Gentiles, they did not have the law of Moses. But for Paul there is no excuse. When Gentiles do what the law requires, they show that 'what the law requires is written on their hearts' (Rom 2:16).

On this basis, morality is not a set of obligations whose only sense lies in the will of the authority figure, and which is not accessible to those beyond the range of that authority. It is, rather, accessible to all because it is part of what we are as moral beings. That does not mean that its demands are easily known, but it does mean that they can be known by all and that they can be justified on their own grounds, without reference to God or religion.

Natural Law and God
Where, then, does God come into the picture? One way of answering this is to speak, not of God, but of the question of God that arises from within our moral experience. The idea of natural law is the idea that reflection can find an order and a direction within human reality. The drives and orientations it finds in the human person suggest there is a purpose to things. The experience of value, and the drive to realise moral values, prompts us to think that the world is not indifferent to the moral struggle. It has been said that moral commitment is 'the womb of hope'. The experience of morality generates the hope

that the order one senses is not a delusion. And this, the question of an ultimate meaningfulness and worthwhileness, is the question of God.

But the sense of a moral order that reason finds in reflecting on nature seems to be contradicted by the further experience of moral negativity. There is the evil in the world and there is the evil in ourselves. There is the persistence of injustice and the repetition through generations of the same cry: why do the wicked prosper and the just suffer? From this the question of God arises in another form, as the question of salvation and justification. Is there mercy for those who sin? Is there justice for those who are dispossessed of their future?

This question of God also makes it clear what we should and should not expect from a religious morality. If all that religion can provide is its own version of the moral law that is already written on all hearts, or further refinements of or additions to the same, then the big questions remain unanswered. However, the morality of the Bible operates at another level, where it offers a response to the question about God, to the question of whether the universe is on our side, to the question of ultimate justice.

In this way we might suggest that it is not so much that God reveals the natural law as that the natural law reveals God. Our reflection on what it is to be a moral being throws up questions that demand God as their answer. A helpful way of looking at the 'moral teachings' of the Bible might be to see it as meeting this demand.

Christian morality can go on from this to speak of God as the foundation of the natural moral law. The traditional way of putting this was to say that the natural law is our participation in the eternal law of God. In other words, when we reflect on our human reality and discover its moral structure, what we are discovering is no less than the plan or design of God. The hope it engenders in us is not in vain.

To say that God is the foundation of the natural law does not mean that God has written into our nature a set of instructions on how to live but simply that God has created us the way we are. It is also to say that God, in creating us the way we are, created freedom. God does not so much tell us what to do, as call us to accept our freedom by discovering what we are, by appreciating what it is to be a human being, and by discerning in concrete situations how to be faithful to and how to realise what we have come to appreciate about ourselves.

The moral laws we then formulate are nothing other than formulations of what freedom has come up with in the process of self-discovery. Thus, to say that God gives us the natural law is to say that God gives us our freedom, as a task and an opportunity.

The Five Approaches

Some concluding comments will relate this discussion of natural law to the four other approaches to morality presented earlier. For, even though we have been presenting natural law as an elaboration of the first way of looking at morality, it has clear links to the other approaches also.

The definition of natural law in terms of reason reflecting on nature makes a clear reference to the understanding of morality as inner conviction. This approach stresses the role of conscience in the personal discovery of and commitment to the moral truth. Not losing sight of this approach will mean that the word 'reason' in the definition is not under-appreciated as it was in the past when the approach to morality as law was seen in isolation.

The approach to morality as personal growth is also intimately connected to the idea of natural law. For the natural law is about our reflections revealing to us the law of our own being – 'law' in the sense of the inner dynamic structure and orientation of the human spirit. What the natural law says in the light of this discovery is: become yourself!

Further elaboration of what the law of our being is will bring us to the fourth and fifth approaches to morality. For that law is most deeply a law of love, whereby we discover or realise ourselves in the gift of ourselves. This logic of love, when transposed to a social context, leads into the language of solidarity and social transformation, where the natural law appears more clearly as the law of our common being, the law of humanity in which we participate.

So, the five approaches continue to interpenetrate. But there is more to it. If each of the five approaches can be seen as contributing to an account of natural law, then each of them can help fill out what has been only hinted at in this chapter. Most of our attention here has focused on natural law as an approach to morality, rather than on what that approach discovers. The chapters that follow can be seen, not only as elaboration of the other ways of looking at morality, but also implicitly as elaborating on what is the natural law of our existence, on what it is to be a human being.

Note
1   Hans Küng and Karl-Josef Kuschel, *A Global Ethic: The Declaration of the Parliament of the World's Religions* (London: SCM Press, 1993).

APPROACHING CHRISTIAN MORALITY

— Vincent MacNamara —

Our question is about the moral or practical dimension of Christianity. That there is a moral dimension we take for granted. We expect a certain kind of life from Christians. We tend to be cynical about those who engage in religious practices but act immorally. We seem, at times, to assume even that the moral activity of Christians should be different from, or better than that of, say, humanists or should contain some plus factor. We would probably want to argue that Christianity had been responsible for safeguarding moral values. And we certainly regard a Christian's moral activity as very important, indeed as decisive, for his or her relationships with God. So much so that Christianity seems to have been dominated by morals. If one were to ask what it means to be a Catholic, it is a fair bet that the answer would be a moral one.

This raises for us questions about how the Christian should understand morality – questions about its source, its criterion, its significance in religion. It would be naive to suggest that there is only one understanding. In the course of history Christianity has seen morality in many different ways. To take only its recent history, we know that, in the period prior to the Council, the emphasis was on God as the author of the moral law, as one who gave commandments. This, in itself, was a departure from an earlier stress on virtue and on the interiority of the new law. In the fifties and sixties there were various attempts to suggest new approaches. Books appeared with titles like *The Law of Christ, The Following of Christ, The Mystical Body and Morality, The Master Calls.* There were attempts to build a morality on the sacraments or on the centrality of charity or on Christ as norm. There was a return to Paul's teaching on the freedom of the sons of God in the new dispensation and to Aquinas's famous treatment of the new law. There was an attempt to relate morality to biblical themes, such as covenant: the Council documents, for example, provide a pastiche of biblical themes. More recently there have been suggestions that we abandon the biblical-centred morality of the Council and insist on the autonomy of morality.

The result, I suspect, is some doubt and confusion about where the Christian should take their stand and about whether they have any solid ground on which to stand. To take some questions: we are constantly being told that a Christian should/should not do X. How am I to understand this? Is it because I am a Christian that I have to act in this way and what of the non-Christian? Is the statement saying something about the content of moral obligation or about its inspiration? Should I do X because God says so, or Christ, or the Bible or the Church? Is this what being moral means?

The problem is to find a starting point that offers the best possibility of understanding morality adequately and of placing it in its religious setting without any diminishment. There are good arguments for starting, not with God or Christ or the Bible, but with the fact of man's moral experience. By that I mean the fact that we are all aware of making distinctions between acts, people, intentions, dispositions, character, etc., which we call good and the opposite which we call evil. If questioned, we are not too clear on what we mean by saying that something is good. This is not just a problem about what kinds of activities are good, but rather about the whole business of calling things good, about what such a word means and why we use it. We have trouble nailing down the moral point of view. But that there is such a point of view on things we have no doubt. It seems that we cannot get on without it. We cannot describe how life presents itself to us. In our daily judgments on ourselves and others we need it. We find that it is rooted in life. If pressed to explain it, we would probably say that it is a conviction we have that there is a kind of life that is fitting and proper for humankind. We do know, I think, that in making moral statements or judgments we are not merely expressing our tastes – it is not arbitrary as the fact that one person likes tomatoes and another doesn't. Nor are we prepared to say that we are merely expressing subjective points of view: we believe there is an objectivity about our statement, for example, that euthanasia is wrong. We believe that there is a truth to be discovered here and that the judgments we make are somehow founded on the natures and relations of things, on the way man is in the world. We would expect to be able to give reasons of some kind for our positions, to justify them. Or, at least, we feel that they are justifiable and that an expert could demonstrate the reasonableness of them.

So deeply engrained in us is this dimension of our experience that it would be difficult for us to live a day without the whole tissue of language of right, wrong, good, bad, duty, obligation, ought, praise, blame and much moral language of a softer kind. This is not to say that we are always in the area of morality when we use such words. 'She ought to be here any minute'; 'He should have taken a seven iron'; 'She is a good philosopher'. These, we know, are not about morality. But compare, 'He ought to treat his wife better'; 'You should not kill'; 'He is a good man'. These are about morality. It is true that there are some fuzzy edges around the area of morality, some points at which we are not sure whether we are making moral judgments or perhaps judgments of good taste. But, by and large, we do know when we are talking morality and when we are not. It is an area that has a high degree of determinateness.

One thing that is clear about moral language and the experience it seeks to express is that it is value language. For that reason it is more difficult and less manageable than fact language. There is, of course, a whole range of value language. We say, for example, that this is a good table or a good typewriter or that a person is a good storyteller or artist or teacher. This is a bit more difficult than saying that this table is four feet long or that the typewriter weighs ten pounds or that the man is five feet ten inches tall. Value language brings in other considerations and begs the question why do you say it is a good table, etc. It involves some kind of criterion, perhaps some discussion about what tables, typewriters, artists are for or are supposed to do. And it leaves open the possibility of disagreement about what is a good table (precisely because people might disagree about what exactly tables are for or how exactly a particular table meets the requirements) in a way in which statements about the length or weight of the table do not. This is something worth remembering when we engage in moral discourse or try to teach morals.

When we are talking the language of morals, we are making evaluations. But we are not evaluating people as good artists or teachers. We need another level of evaluation. We recognise that one may be a good artist but a bad person or a bad teacher but a good person. We recognise that a person might become more developed intellectually and culturally – and so at that level a better person – if they were to desert their spouse and family and devote themselves to improving their mind. But we would probably say that they ought not to do it. So we accept that they become a better person at one level – the moral – although they are diminished at another. We are saying that pleasure or profit or intellectual development are not decisive but that they are to be integrated into living and that we have some idea about how this is to be done. There is an overriding judgment to be made. It is the kind of judgment that has enabled thinkers since Plato down to say that it is better to suffer injustice than to commit it. It is the kind of starkly simple judgment that is often made at the end of a person's life: 'He was a good man' (which is not simply about whether he pursued pleasure or profit or the development of himself but it not unrelated to them) or, 'She was a good doctor but a terrible woman'.

This is our moral experience. Let us call it the moral fact: it is very much a fact of life. We might adopt James Mackey's description of it in his book, *Life and Grace* (Dublin, 1966). It contains, he says, two elements. First, we are aware of making distinctions between conduct we call good and conduct we call evil. Second, we are aware of the peculiar psychological phenomenon that there is attached a sense of obligation to do the good and avoid the evil. If you want to call it conscience, that is fine. Or the natural law, if by that you mean what Aquinas meant when he said that the first principle of the natural law was that good should be done and evil avoided. I take it that he was not saying that we go around telling ourselves this. But that it is our experience that we distinguish good and bad conduct and know that there is an obligation to do the one and avoid the other. We know that all sorts of people in all ages and cultures recognise this moral point of view. They may, of course, differ from us in their understanding of it, in the content they give to it. But they agree with us on the fact that life is not be be lived arbitrarily, that it matters how one does it. Some will accept that a man may have ten wives, for example. But they are his wives and nobody else's. That determines his relation to them and the relation of others to him and to them.

In doing morality we are concerning ourselves with one of the great questions of life: how are we to live? Which is also the question: who are we, what are we? It is a question that has troubled humans from the beginning. It is not something that we make but rather something that we find and to which we must submit, if we are to find peace with ourselves. It makes a claim on us. Although it arises within us, it is not something that we can manipulate: in this sense it is greater than we are. Some would like to say that it has a sacred character about it, that it is religious. I take it that by this they mean that it is perceived and experienced by us as something of importance and dignity, something to which we must attend or pay the price of feeling that we have not been true to ourselves. A fair amount of our expression of ourselves in song and story has been a recognition of this. If we cherish certain classic statements of it, either in philosophy or in literature generally, it is because we find that the writer has successfully caught and illuminated something that is common to all of us but that we cannot easily articulate.

What is important is that we recognise this moral experience in ourselves and others and take it as the starting point of our understanding. If we are teachers or preachers of morality, we must enable people to appreciate that morality is something that is native to us, that we make moral distinctions of our own accord, that we simply find that we need it. In teaching, what we are trying to do is help people to understand themselves. We sometimes feel ourselves burdened with the task of convincing people about moral positions, as if we had somehow made morality or were responsible for it. It is not religion that has made morality, not the Church, not even God, except in the sense that He has made us. So we should not see ourselves as importing morality into the lives of others. Morality does not start with the teacher but with the pupil. Our role is to awaken them to and help them come to terms with their own question about how one is to live one's life. It is a question that is as old as humankind and no one can afford to belittle it or treat it lightly. One wants to make contact with the question in the pupil. This can be done even with the rebellious. Because, while they may reject particular statements of morality, they will insist that they be treated morally. For example, they will object to being bullied or treated harshly or unfairly. They are rightly saying that there is a way for people to live together. This, too, is the central message for the moral educator. He or she can take it from there.

What we are talking about here, obviously, is the basis or source of morality. Nobody doubts that there will be differences about the implications of this, about principles. But, long before that stage is reached, there can be some agreement on what morality is all about and on the original source of principles. At this level, at least, we can be seen to make sense to people.

All of this is insisting on the autonomy of morality. By this we mean that morality makes its own demand: one should be moral because one should be moral. The question, 'why be moral?' (and the question presupposes that the questioner is open to reason, otherwise they have no business asking it) receives as its first answer: because it is the rational thing to do. So morality does not immediately need religion; one does not need God before becoming aware of moral obligation. It is true that a religion, like any other group, may have arrived at certain conclusions about how one is to be moral and may have its own understanding of the ultimate significance of morality. But, even if religion is abandoned, the person is still left with the moral question, unless humanity is also to be abandoned. It is true that if there were no God there would be no morality, because we would not exist. And one can certainly speak of morality as the will of God, provided one is aware of the limited nature of such language. But God is no more the author of the principles of morality than He is the author of the principles of logic. Morality is a human thing. Neither does morality depend on reward. There are many fine moral people, who do not believe in God or in heaven. But they do believe in being moral. For them virtue is its own reward, i.e. the knowledge that they are living in the way in which they believe people should live. They are not slow to point out that, if they treat their fellows well, it is because they believe in the value and the dignity of the other and not simply because someone has told them to do it or because they hope for any reward for doing so. They will accuse religious morality of being anti-morality or of being infantile. We would want to argue that it is possible for religion to integrate morality into itself and enrich it with its own vision, without impairing its purity in any way. But that is another day's work.

Our question is one of approach. There are arguments in favour of different starting points. But it seems to me that emphasising moral experience is most likely to give the true understanding of morality. This is not just a matter of tactics. It is a matter of what morality is all about. If a student, for example, does not understand that morality is a human thing, if he is led to believe that it has only to do with being a Christian, then he has misunderstood it. If he somehow has the impression that morality is something that begins outside him, that someone else imposes on him, he is mistaken. And if he has picked up the idea that morality is something one accepts if he wishes to ensure one's future happiness, he has devalued it. It is easy to have such notions in a religious morality. It is easy to operate with the idea that one has to be moral, because God has made moral laws, much as a human legislator makes them. This would be to misunderstand both morality and God: it is bad for both. For that reason one has to be careful with the God-commandments-reward model of morality. It tends to reduce morality to obedience to the will of another. But morality cannot be just a matter of doing what one is told, even by God. And moral response involves more than doing things, performing physical acts. It involves intention, understanding, knowing what one is doing and why. And, in particular, knowing that what one is doing is being human and that this is the first reason why one should do it. If our aim is the freedom of the Christian moral person, we might heed the advice of Aquinas: 'He, therefore, who avoids evil, not because it is evil but because of the command of God is not free, but he who avoids evil because it is evil is free'. The aim, therefore, must be some understanding of the source of morality and some personal appropriation of values. It raises questions about what we are trying to do in communicating or teaching morality. But more about that another time.

It would be a mistake to think about this moral experience in a totally individual way. One learns morality in community, as one learns everything else: it is part of the wisdom of the community. It would equally be a mistake to regard it as a merely formal experience, with which one is born and which must later be filled in. It is experience in situations. One sometimes hears the objection that the approach suggested is saying that everyone is to be their own moral guide, a law unto themselves. It is not saying this: our concern is with the source of moral obligation and the basic meaning of principles and commandments. The problem still remains of finding the right answer to the question of how we are to live. But it is important to realise that the whole paraphernalia of morality – the whole panoply of values, rules, commandments and the explorations of meta-ethics – is an attempt to understand the experience. For the individual, the task of the moral life is to listen to the experience, to grow in openness to it and let it lead. To do the truth. For the community, the task is to enable the individual to accept it, to interpret it aright and to be able to respond to it. This is the educator's role also. It is a worthy vocation.

We are not humanists and what I have been discussing is far from our total vision of the human or of morality. But there is this core to morality. There is everything to be gained from pausing to reflect on it as a relatively independent part of our experience, before one introduces considerations of a religious kind. In this way we are more likely to disentangle the strands. However we are to relate it to, or understand it within the religious context, it must be in a way that respects its self-consistency and gives it its full value as a human phenomenon.

CHRISTIAN FAITH
AND MORALITY

—— Vincent MacNamara ——

The connection of faith and morals is not immediately obvious. It is true that we expect faith to be expressed in action. We assume that there is something hypocritical or unthinking about one who prays and worships but who does not bother about moral living. Many of us even identify faith with morality. Having faith is often taken to mean having a particular set of morals. When we say that someone has lost the faith we often mean that he/she has abandoned Church morality. Or worse still, that he/she has abandoned its canon law – has given up weekly Mass-going, for example, or refuses to observe the Church's law on marriage. More recently, theologians of liberation have insisted that faith is praxis. It is worth reminding ourselves, however, that the Gospel injunction was to repent and believe the Gospel, the good news. How or why this is related to morality, or to what morality is, raises interesting and complex questions.

The first set of questions is the more crucial for Christianity, the 'how' or 'why' questions, i.e. the place which moral life has in Christianity. The institution of morality is as old as humankind. It is found before and outside of Judaeo-Christianity. It is an area of experience that can be distinguished from the area of religious faith. What does it have to do with or what is its relation to Christian faith? What is the relationship between the categories and language of morality – good, bad, right, wrong, virtue, obligation – and the categories and language of Christian proclamation – salvation, grace, sin, damnation? I do not want to pursue that question here. Except to say, in passing, that many Roman Catholics have a very simple view of it. The link between faith and morals is forged from them by belief in a God who has given us moral commands which are the way to and the condition of beatific vision. This does not appear to me to be a very felicitous way of understanding things. I cannot dwell on that here but it is important because the model which we have of that relationship will deeply affect our understanding of Christianity. It will shape our understanding of God and of the relationship between God and ourselves. It is not surprising that different version of it have produced the most decisive and disastrous split in the history of Christianity.

It is the second question, however, the 'what morality' question, that chiefly interests me here. Morality seems to come inevitably and early as part of the faith-package. Disciples asked Jesus: 'Master, what am I to do to possess eternal life?' John's disciples had asked him. Those who heard the message of Paul asked him. John the Evangelist seems to have encouraged his disciples almost to identify believing and doing. James did certainly. Doing, however, is not to be confined to moral doing. Before one arrives at the doing of morality there is a doing that is basic to faith: it is the being/doing of faith-attitudes. To believe the Gospel of Jesus, to share his faith is, we are told, a conversion. But not only a moral conversion. It is a new way of seeing life that makes all things new. It is an enriched perspective that makes the difference between meaning and meaninglessness, between joy and fear, between hope and doubt.

Faith and Vision

Such faith-conversion is foundational for the Christian. It is what makes him/her a particular kind of person. It shapes his consciousness, his imagination, his loyalties. When we ask about his moral life we must do so in the light of this faith-experience. Moral judgments are not made in a vacuum. They are made by particular persons, and by groups with a particular world-view and cohesion. The beliefs of Christianity enter into such judgments. Or, if you like, the myths, symbols, stories. The current rage of talking about Christianity in terms of story is, I think, more than a passing fashion. Dogmatic statements do not catch the imagination or engage the spirit as stories do. They do not get into the bloodstream of an individual or a people in the same way. Our ballads and our songs are so much more powerful in creating the national consciousness than our Constitution. So too with faith-consciousness. The Jews did not hand on a set of beliefs. They told stories. What they told to their children and recalled in their assemblies was that God had chosen them, taught them, delivered them, brought them into a land and promised them even greater joys, including the coming of a definitive redeemer. It was a long story, recounted through the generations. It was a formative one. It made a people with a particular ethos, a feel about themselves, an attitude to others, a way of looking at the future. Above all it made, if gradually, a people with a basic confidence in life and in death, in sorrow and in success, even in failure and persecution.

The Christians are the heirs to that story but the event of which they could tell was so strikingly different that they saw themselves as a different people. What they knew was that the God of the long centuries of fidelity had so loved the world that He had sent his Son, that this Son was born of our flesh, that he lived and joyed and suffered among and with us. They told that

MORAL THEOLOGY

his godliness shone through in his trust in his Father, in his love for each poor one, in his rejection of power, in his courage to go against the privilege of the age, in his fidelity to his vision even at the cost of death. They were told that he had gone to God in resurrection, a sign and a guarantee of the final hope of his followers. They rejoiced that in this knowledge all had been made new for them. Life was graced: all was held in the care of God. Nothing, neither death nor life, could take that away from them. The point about such faith-stories is that they cut to the quick – if we take them seriously. They involve our sense of ourselves at a deep level, our basic philosophy of life, our stance about who we are and where we come from and how we stand in the universe and where we are going and what it means to be whole.

What, then, as the disciples asked, are we to do? First of all, we are to let the stories of creation and liberation, of annunciation and sending, of dying and rising seep into our lives. We are to take our bibles and let the conviction come true for us that reality is accepting, that life is a gift, that we are of more value than many sparrows, that the seed dying brings forth fruit, that in the man Jesus going quietly to his death is our hope, that in the cross is resurrection. If we could feel all of that we would be some way into morality. Some way not only to doing but to seeing. By seeing I mean understanding, judging what one should do, what shape of life is consonant with being a Christian. It is the Christian, this Bible person and not any other, who is looking for the way. It is the view of the landscape through his particular lens that interest us. We might call it the Christian imagination, the composite picture of life as the Christian sees it, the Christian *Gestalt*.

We are not the first Christians. We are in continuity with the imagination of Paul and Ambrose and Augustine and with the folk at Ephesus and Rome and Glendalough. We share the same ethos, the same basic configuration of thought. Different times, different places, different problems, it is true. So there cannot be any facile recourse to Paul for solutions. The centuries have brought their wisdom too. Solutions of an age when slavery and the inferior state of women were too much of a good thing to trouble Christian vision are not solutions now. It was clearly too much to ask Paul to be impervious to the prejudices of his age and culture even when the inner thrust of Christianity pointed in another direction. (Though even in the midst of such moral shortcoming you can find shafts of light, pick up something of the ethos: 'Wives obey your husbands *in the Lord* ...')

So the relation of faith to morality is not found by looking for precise solutions of a practical order in the Bible – laws or precepts that are eternally valid. That cannot be. One would have to filter biblical precepts through so many objections that any argument of the form, 'It says in the Bible ...' will be found to be still-born. You cannot regard the Bible as a code of ethics. You cannot simply dip into it and pull out precise moral rules. There are, of course, moral statements in the Bible with which one agrees. Equally, there are statements with which one cannot agree. So appeal to the Bible as a moral authority must be treated with circumspection. But it is still important. Biblical faith does bear on morality but it does so indirectly rather than directly. We must do our thinking afresh today but we do so in conversation with the apostolic Church and its problems. We try to catch the dynamic of ethos and ethic that prevailed with them. It should prevail with us. But for us it is a matter of putting today's problems, in today's world, with today's knowledge, to our faith – in the realisation that it has been done before with a different set of problems and presuppositions in a different world. We are not to be slaves to the limited past. But neither is it without a message for us.

Towards Moral Decisions

What we can hope to do in our own day and try to do here is to plot some general directions in which decisions lie for the Christian. Let us not think primarily of laying down a set of rules which purport to catch the heart of the Christian moral life. Our decisions are unique and unrepeatable. Our moral lives are not about the Ten Commandments but about the quirks and twists of life that we meet in the raw towns that we believe and die in. They are more likely to be about how easy it is to be bitter or envious, to feather one's own nest, to look after number one, to be enclosed in one's own ambitions or those of one's family, to harbour resentment, to make people nasty offers which they cannot refuse. They are about temptation to self-aggrandisement of a political or sexual or intellectual kind, about taking advantage, about cheating, about hoarding, about not being fond enough of the right to refuse the expedient. They are about sneaking your own way, aligning God's will with your own, respecting riches, not wanting to know your poor relations. About such one cannot easily elaborate rules. But one can indicate some of the great shaping thrusts of the Christian spirit which should guide us in decisions.

One of the most basic thrusts that enters into my thinking about morality is the conviction that Christianity does not deny but assumes into itself all that is greatest and most delicate of the human spirit. That comes to me in the stories that God saw that the world was good, that Christ became flesh with us, that he rejoiced in corn and wine and friends, that he was lonely, that he hated to lose his life, that he was afraid of the unknown, that he could not keep back tears when he saw the poor suffer. He was, as Paul said, The Man. Or, as John Paul II said, the One who reveals the human person to himself/herself. The stories are encapsulated for me in the theological axiom that grace does not destroy but supposes nature or in the phrase of

Irenaeus that the glory of God is the person fully alive. I have trouble nowadays in disentangling the nature-grace bit. But it gives me huge confidence that whatever has meant most to the dignity and flourishing of the human person since the dawn of history must not be lost to Christianity. This demands that I will expect to find in Christian morality the questioning, the unrest for the truth, the ancient love of learning that has marked human civilisation. I will expect to come on a deep vein of concern for liberty, equality and fraternity, of respect for the autonomy and responsibility of the human person. I will be wondering if I find a fear of discussion or a too facile recourse to authoritative assertion. I will be disappointed if I do not meet a compassionate realism, a sympathy and a keen sense of the opaqueness of much of what we have to live through. I will not anticipate easy answers. I know that we cannot flee the complexities of life and that we cannot absolve ourselves from the task of teasing out moral argument in just such complexities. I know that we must test everything, that there are no hot lines to God, no instant Ceefax from the Spirit and no virtue in fuzzy appeals to scripture. God works in us through human means. He has given us the task of discerning our lives. To discern, I suppose, is to think well.

Much of this is shared with all people of good-will. It should be assumed when we say that we discern as Christians, In fact, advertence to the universal phenomenon of morality helps us to get the focus of our moral thinking right: it is, at least, one of the useful *praenotanda* to moral theology. But there is much more for us to do as Christians. We can declare our right and responsibility to make our judgments in fidelity to our whole story. We share the faith, the choices. It should emerge that our perceptions, our evaluations, the facts of the case for us, the prominence we give to some facts rather will all be coloured by our particular imagination. What will our vision yield? We seem to have difficulty in spelling out what faith in action would look like. And yet, if there is anything to our talk about Christian values we should be able to do so.

It would be naive, I suppose, to romanticise about the early Church – it had its share of rakes. And we have seen that it would be a mistake to try to apply its solutions without qualification to today. But the melody does linger on. We find it hard to rid ourselves of the nostalgia that ethos did then shape ethic and that Church life has since hardened into something from which Gospel freshness has vanished. When we ask about Christian values, about faith and morals, we are trying to recapture that spirit. We are asking about the same imagination pursued into behaviour today. We are looking for lives fresh with evangelical outlook in our times, for Gospel people.

I think I know them when I see them. What seems most crucial and most decisive for their ethic is their basic vision, their key image. The God of whom their story tells holds their lives together, gives them anchorage. 'The Lord is my rock.' 'Teach us to care and not to care.' Faith in God determines meaning for them. It gives a perspective of which most of us fall short. It shapes judgment. Most of us have insecure moorings. We want and fret so much. We will feel happy or good or fulfiled if we have or reach or hold or possess or can show or can prove. The goods, ends, states of affair which we desire, i.e. our values, are puny because our vision is puny. They are out of harmony with the story. We flirt all the time with what the faith of Jesus tells us is not our growth and flourishing, not the things that are to our peace. We are constantly being told that we are an acquisitive society and that there is no hope for the country unless we change. But how to change? The question is how we are to educate our desires, how we can reverse or modify our values, how we can *recta sapere*. I am not just talking about being able to do what we know we should do. It is a question even of seeing. A grasping society we will remain and we will not see any point in anything else unless we can persuade ourselves and our children that in God the true value is offered to us. Unless we can convince ourselves, can see inwardly, that faith in Him and union with Him make us whole, and that such wholeness does not require many of the lesser goods and is even put at risk by them.

If you take this seriously you will, of course, be largely on your own. You will have to hold quietly to your own overarching vision of the good life. You will have to allow by your eyes and ears what the consumer society regards as the things that are to your peace, and what the television advertisements tell you will make you a beautiful person. You will let them pass for fear, as the scriptures have it, of losing your soul, your true self – your integrity, your wholeness, your serenity. If you do so, do not think that you are the victim of petty piety or of the opium of religion. You are engaging in moral judgment, perhaps in the greater morality of which D.H. Lawrence wrote: there is a little morality, he said, which concerns the little needs of persons and a greater morality which is often in conflict with it but which concerns greater needs, greater truths about the person. You might differ with him about the nature of it but you are on the right track. You are entitled to your vision.

We pursue it further. I take from the faith of Jesus, as distinct from dualist and apocalyptic world views, an immediate commitment to this world, a concern for life and bread and freedom. But it was not the whole of his story. Man does not live on bread alone – Christians are somehow to integrate that into their lives. Someone I know recently gave away his car and what little luxuries he possessed. It was not an act of almsgiving. That was not the way he saw it (and therefore not the act which he did). He did not give to the poor. It was, I presume, a piece of conduct that derived from some wider than usual notion of wholeness, blessedness, personal creativity. It was meant to accentuate religious values and make them more vividly present. It is, I suppose, something of the idea of detachment that runs through the Christian tradition. Poverty is a variation on it. One needs freedom for religious things. One should so conduct oneself in human affairs as not to forget divine things. One should not be so seduced by the physical as to forget the metaphysical, as to allow the faith-dimension to become dimmed. One should insist with oneself on the total meaning of life: development and comfort at a certain level may have to be sacrificed to one's total vision.

All of this says something about the horizon of our evaluations, about the Christian's faith-vision of the meaning of the person and about its view of true flourishing. It is the same basic faith as gave rise to many of the Gospel parables about riches, to the injunctions to be in the world but not of it and to seek first the kingdom of God. I am not saying that one can take such Gospel injunctions literally. Nor that one can say as a general rule that the kingdom is more likely to be discovered by fleeing the world than by passionate commitment to its development. But there are directions here for the shaping of life: there is an abiding wisdom in such Gospel maxims. The Christian today finds a relation between ethos and ethic that has resonances in the life of the apostolic community.

Perhaps trust is another general direction for our lives: it relates to stories which we have about the providence of God, to sayings about the grass of the field and about fathers who know how to give fish to their children. It is not just about the stance one takes to suffering and disappointment. It is just as surely related to action and enterprise. It has enabled some to undertake a life that on a secular calculation might have been regarded as imprudent or as not providing sufficiently for the future. And not just to undertake it but to make a judgment about the appropriateness of such a life and even about one's responsibility to opt for it.

Detachment, poverty, trust. There is close to them what I can only call a Christian humility. It arises delicately out of one's belief in God as creator, sustainer, giver of all good things – which engenders a sense of reverence and thankfulness. The believer knows that he/she is not the most important being in the world. He knows that all are subject to the reign of God, that all life is stewardship, that all history is in His hands, that the ultimate judgment on human events is not bounded by this world. He knows that none of us lives to himself only and none of us dies for himself only; but that if we live it is for the Lord that we live and if we die it is for the Lord that we die (Rom 14:7). This gives rise to a distinctive bearing, to a modest and humble behaviour. It makes sense of the advice: 'There must be no room for rivalry or personal vanity among you, but you must humbly reckon others better than yourselves. Look to each other's interest and not merely to your own. Let your bearing towards one another arise out of your life in Christ Jesus: for the divine nature was his from the first, yet he did not think to snatch at equality with God (Phil 2:3 ff.).

The Interests of Others
I suppose Christian faith will issue above all in that remarkable revolution in which Paul's directive rings true that we should look to the interests of others and not to our own (1 Cor 10:24). How can one make sense of this, let alone be able to do it? Some have said that the human person will always be wolf to his neighbour, some that altruistic action is never anything but disguised self-interest, some that the best one can hope for is an implicit non-aggression pact with others – but never any

genuine love. Much of the best of morality has been built on concern for fairness and impartiality and most of us would be happy if we had the imagination and generosity to carry through what that demands – do as you would be done unto. But Christianity goes much further: 'Give to everyone who asks'; 'There must be no limit to your goodness'; 'You should be ready to lay down your lives for one another'; 'You must wash each other's feet.' It can demand this because it offers to change the focus of our attentions and fears. We are, first, to repent, to believe the Gospel of acceptance and forgiveness for ourselves. It is only if we do so, only from this new perspective, that Gospel talk of seeking the good of others, rather than our own, will make good moral sense. It is because we are coffined in ourselves, because we suffer the basic insecurity of humankind, that we fight so self-righteously for our fair share and react so viciously if we think someone is getting the better of us (and not because of some almighty concern for a moral principle of fairness). A care for oneself is morally right. But we cannot think of ourselves out of relation to the various communities in which we live. Our lives are so intertwined that decisions about ourselves are almost always decisions about others. So one might wonder about the cult of personal development that is sometimes put forward as an entirely justifiable and obvious choice. There might be a real question about the criterion of morality that is implied here. As far back as Aristotle there is a close relation between virtue and community. The Christian ethic is strongly communitarian ('We are free to do anything but does everything help the building of the community? Each of you must regard not his own interests but the other man's'), strong on self-forgetfulness and at its best has a position on the option between self and others.

The point is often made that the morality of the Sermon on the Mount presumes the Gospel of the kingdom (ethos and ethic). What we are talking about here will more likely be a real option for one who can accept that he/she has been delivered by Christ. Delivered not just from loneliness, not just from fear about the future and from insecurity. But also from the repression and inhibition which locks us in, which makes us afraid of others, worried about what they will think, fearful of making mistakes, prickly about criticism, threatened by the charm or wit or grace of success of others – a combination that is the source of a fair amount of our immorality. Sure anchorage could help, the secure harbour of faith. I could be the source of a genuine – and critically important – self-esteem. That does not absolve us from seeking God's gifts to iron out whatever it is within us that tends to make us see the other as threat rather than as gift. It should rather encourage us to look for the healing which Paul saw as among the gifts of the community. Nor does it mean that moral judgments or decisions will be easy or will not sometimes present a most complex face. But it does give us a different perspective on ourselves and others. It gives a friendly space in which to see things. Faith, they say, is 'seeing as'. Seeing yourself as accepted and forgiven by God can transform your vision. It can make you a different person. That is grace. A person who reads the whole landscape of life in this experience will be likely to make different judgments from the one who reads it in the experience of bitterness and threat and wounding. Beauty is supposed to be in the eye of the beholder. Moral truth appears to be in the heart and imagination of the beholder.

The Logic of Christian Morality

Much recent writing has made the point that faith is performative, that it is illogical to go on believing in a caring God, who is known as Father of the poor, if one does not do something about the condition of the poor. The converse is also true and perhaps this is even more crucial: the God in whom we believe is known not from our talk but from our actions. If one is without a care for others, if the faith-community is not a caring community, then the outsider must wonder in whom or in what they believe. The logic of Christian morality is expressed in the first letter of John, what Cullmann called the catechesis of the morality of the New Testament: 'This is the love I mean; not our love for God but God's love for us; since God has loved us so much we too should love one another' (1 John 4:10). Or as both John and Paul put it: if Christ has laid down his life for us, then we should be ready to lay down our lives for the brethren. The other point also appears. Believing in the Son of God and loving the brethren are inseparable for John. One who fails to love the other is as surely in the dark as one who does not believe in the Son. The former is on to the wrong god as surely as is the latter. He does not know who God is. It is not surprising that love for the other is then seen as a necessary sign of credibility, as a mark of the true Church. 'May they be one ... you who sent me ...' (Jn 17:23). This story of a God who loves and of a Jesus who died for love is what we recount every time we celebrate. It is this that we try to allow into our hearts. It is the subversive memory which is to haunt us every time we commemorate: 'Calling to mind the life, death and resurrection ...' It ought to be illogical to go on recalling that and not begin to be aware of the shape which life with others should take. Unfortunately, we do manage the illogicality.

We must go further. There is talk in Christianity about bearing the cross. The symbol of the cross, the death-resurrection, hangs over Christianity. It is not a matter of opting out; neither is it the cowardice or weakness of which Nietzsche complained. It is that the experience of Jesus is taken to have something to say to the situation of every human being. Much moral writing seems to envisage situations of logic and clarity in which we are dealing with perfectly reasonable people. But we live in a world in which justice will not be done, in which rights will not be allowed, in which goodness will not be rewarded, in which evil prospers. A fair slice of life is about personal injustice and about situations which have injustice written into them. It is certainly of the greatest importance that Christians see their call to be in the struggle for justice – not for reasons of strategy but for reasons of truth. But the struggle for justice is not straightforward: it gives rise to complex questions. The meaning of justice will not be agreed upon – for example, think of how difficult it has been for the 'two sides' in Northern Ireland to agree on what is a just solution? And even if the meaning of justice could be agreed worldwide, justice will not be done. In such situations there must still be a Christian response. The unqualified demand for justice is not the whole of the Christian message. Christianity is not only about the struggle for justice but about how one is to react when justice is not being done and is not likely to be done.

There are those who think that the Christian response sometimes suggests self-sacrifice, non-resistance, not vindicating oneself, enduring injustice. The Lutheran pastor, Helmut Gollwitzer, threw away his gun and said that he was not prepared to engage in the logic of violence. The logic of violence is that you insist on your rights at any price, that you get your enemy before he gets you. The logic of early Christianity seemed to be otherwise: do not repay evil with evil but repay evil with good; you must love your enemies and do good to those who hate you; forgive your enemies as God in Christ forgave you. Such judgments are supposed to make sense to us. It is not always easy to plot the exact entailment here from faith to practice but there undoubtedly enters into their making Christian belief in providence and the value of union with God, the hope of fulfilment in a hereafter, and the conviction that in Christ's death-resurrection there is a clue to human blessedness.

The professional moralist might argue the toss about some of this. He might say that morality is about solutions to practical problems, that what we have been discussing here belongs too much to one's inner life, that it is religion rather than morality, that it pertains to the domain of personal vocation and ideal rather than to universalizable moral rules. The points can be met – but only briefly here. I would argue that the directions for living considered here belong in some measure to every Christian life and are not for an elite. I take it, too, that if we are interested in conduct we are concerned for more then external observable action. A person's vision, his desires, the configuration of his thought, the dispositions of his heart all interest us. They must make a large part of what one means by a person. How a person does what he does interests us too. As does the reason why one judges a particular course to be the right course. Likewise, the desires with which one acts, the motives, the description under which an act is performed, are all relevant. All of these, I know, are technical terms and must not be thrown around lightly. But neither are they to be neglected. They enter into moral action and the more one takes account of them the more it will be seen how Christian vision subtly affects moral life. Vision gives rise to values. Values found attitudes, perspectives and dispositions. They, in turn, issue in and accompany action. It is in the totality that faith expresses itself.

Creative Responsibility

I don't want this article to go soft on me. I don't want it to dissolve in a romantic blur – even a romantic Christian blur. I am not in any sense underestimating the difficulty. Isn't it better to be honest and aware of failure than to play down the call? My main point is that one's world-view should enter into and does make a difference to judgment and action. Moral life should not be detached from one's basic story. It may be said that other world-views will yield judgments analogous to those which appear to be consonant with Christianity. Very well. I am not concerned to prove the specificity of Christian ethics. That is a complex question and I agree that it is of importance. I am only saying that the Christian should do morality in fidelity to his/her vision and ethos.

That does not mean that it is not possible and important to give a credible account of how judgments are reached. It is not a justification for overlooking the general grammar of moral discourse. The process of moral argument is hard-headed, although it requires imagination and sensitivity. I suspect decisions that can only be justified by appeal to the Spirit or to the now too-common 'I have prayed about it'. Christian intuitionism can hardly be any more respectable than any other kind. There must be a rationality about judgments. But one can, I think, fairly call it a Christian rationality. I mean that the Christian is entitled to be faithful to his basic philosophy. If he is, he will find that there is a sense in which the facts of life are different for him and that as a result the common concepts of morality – welfare, harm, good, perfection, flourishing – are affected in interesting ways. This does not mean a ghetto morality. There will be considerable coincidence with some non-Christian moralities and there will be the possibility of large agreement in matters of public policy. But there will be times when personal choice is explicable precisely in terms of Christian faith.

One could describe such morality as the following of Jesus or as discipleship. That is fine provided it does not imply that there can be a simple translation of what Jesus did to the present day. And provided that it is not understood to imply that one can find easy answers by asking 'What would Jesus do?'. Discipleship is a matter rather of trying to enter into the faith of Jesus in one's situation today and allowing it to suggest general values and orientations. It is of such that I have been writing, not giving solutions, but sketching the directions in which solutions lie. One could, indeed, try to set some kind of fence around this individual Christian moral life – what have been called 'rock-bottom duties' or what Jews and Christians refer to as the decalogue. That kind of enterprise is useful and necessary for the community: it gives rise to the common moral rules. But to do this is only to stake out the territory within which each one will live the drama of his own personal responsibility. You cannot catch much of life in the net of a rules morality. Most of it will slip through its wide mesh. There is no substitute for creative responsibility.

Faith then affects vision. It carries in train its own proper values, aims and intention. It enters into judgment – the lonely judgment of the individual, the public stance of the community. It accompanies action. Not only that, but to the Christian today it offers its own history – the history, ragged and struggling at times, of the ethos pursued into action in the Bible, in the tradition of the community, in the lives of the just. Faith is far from being a solvent for all our problems. In fact it commits us to be honest about difficulties, not to pretend, to take seriously the *Schadenfreude*, to accept the paradox of the half-beast, half-angel. There are problems about which it will tell us nothing and about which we might get better advice outside the Christian fold. It tells us nothing about the principle of double effect. It is no help in the agony of the choice of life against life. It has nothing to say about when life begins or about what is to be regarded as human, any more than it has about how the planets came to be or what is the cure for cancer. It tells us nothing about the conscience problem of education in mixed marriages. It says nothing about methods of contraception. But it has suggestive things to say about trust in God, about humble bearing, about passion for others, about forgetfulness of self, about tolerance, fidelity and enduring patience. It has cleansing things to say to those who confuse wealth and power with wholeness and blessedness, or who identify easy gratification with ultimate joy. It has an aversion to filling your barns, ensuring the first places, calling down fire from heaven, making a fetish of Church laws, taking your sword from your scabbard, having your hand kissed in the market-place.

Paul was so convinced of the cohesive power of this faith – one Lord, one faith, one baptism – that he was optimistic that we could discern together, solve disputes, agree on courses of action. 'Agree with one another after the manner of Christ Jesus, so that with one mind and one voice you may praise the God and Father of our Lord Jesus Christ' (Rom 5:15). '... If then our common life in Christ yields anything to stir the heart, any loving consolation, any sharing of the Spirit, any warmth of affection or compassion, fill up my cup of happiness by thinking and feeling alike, with the same love for one another, the same turn of mind, and a common care for unity' (Phil 2:1). Too optimistic, perhaps. Good decisions are not easily made. It is technically difficult to marshal all of the relevant facts, to understand the situation aright. It is practically difficult to be open to this. The willingness to know the truth is not to be taken for granted. There is so much in us that prevents us from honest judgment – fears, self-pity, prejudice, self-will. We cheat and rationalise. We hustle out the considerations that should be listened to. We shout down the quiet appeals of truth. We do not achieve the stillness in which the breath of God is heard. We do not pray long enough to let the mud settle in the unquiet pools of our lives. St Thomas knew that it is only the good who judge well – those who are not afraid of what might be asked, who are completely open to discovery. Most of us are afraid of the unknown and unable to leave the comfortable nest of our lives – poor enough, perhaps, but familiar. If only we could allow faith to lead us out to the broad, sunlit uplands.

Context, Motivation, Strength

All of that is in outline only, and is only part of the way in which faith bears on morality. It is what mostly interests people when the issue is raised. It is the 'What are we to do?' part. There is much more room for only three brief points. The first is that for the person of faith the whole of morality receives a new context and significance. From Moses to our own day the Judaeo-Christian story tells that response to God is mediated through the daily struggle to answer the moral claim. From then until now morality has been gradually seen as part of the covenant relationship, of the following of Christ, of life in the Spirit. So that the message which finally comes to us is that the relationship is so organic that to be in union with the neighbour is to be in union with God, to be in the light, to be in salvation space.

The second is that faith gives to morality not only enlightenment but a structure of support and hope. One who believes in a God of rational purpose, one who has stories about a kingdom to be created, and ancient promises to be realised, has a warrant and endorsement for the whole moral enterprise. One whose sagas are of the power and undying providence of God has a hope for his undertakings even when they appear to be frustrated by events. If the Lord build the house they do not labour in vain who seek to build it. There is a courage to carry on in spite of evil and death and destruction that sometimes overtake the noblest creations of the human spirit – 'Even though the flocks vanish from the folds and stalls stand empty of cattle ...'

The third has to do with Paul's cry in his weakness for help from some quarter. 'The good that I would I do not do ... Who will deliver me?' Part of our problem is not in the knowing but in the doing. We often know what to do but we experience the gap of our weakness or selfishness or inconstancy. *'Lava quod est sordidum, riga quod est aridum, sana quod est saucium; flecte quod est rigidum, fove quod est frigidum, rege quod est devium.'* There is no shortage of realism there: our father in the faith knew all about moral waywardness. (A pity that we have bartered the long, cool cadences of that hymn for a mess of kitsch.)

Our story is meant to be a strength. Perhaps it is its motivational (encouraging/parenetic) power that is the most significant element in biblical morality. Here is preaching a-plenty. We have seen the great dynamic in John – 'If God has loved us ...'. This indicative-imperative motif runs through the whole Bible as stimulus and inspiration. It is easy to sketch the portrait of a Christian, easier still to lay down the law to him/her. Telling people to be moral and helping them to do so are two different operations. We have not attended much to the second, to moral education. Our biblical tales are one source of help. Read, for example, Philippians 2, Colossians 3, Galatians 5, Romans 6 and 8, John 13. We need to harness all the power of the story, let it find its way into the valleys of our lives, warm the cockles of our hearts. But, again, it takes time and thought and prayer.

Above all, through all the striving, we are to keep the composition of our picture right. It is easy to lose perspective. We do so if we think that moral striving is entitlement. When we have done everything we are to say that we are unprofitable servants. There must be no diminishing of grace and mercy. He has reconciled us. That is our faith-story. We can only try to respond.

FORMING AND FOLLOWING ONE'S CONSCIENCE

— Linda Hogan —

One of the interesting features of Irish debates about questions such as the decriminalisation of homosexual acts or the legalisation of contraception or divorce is the ambiguity of the Irish public regarding moral responsibility. While on the one hand personal responsibility is both recognised and valued, on the other there seems to be a desire for certainty and simplicity. Indeed I have been repeatedly struck to hear teachers of religion in secondary schools say that while young adults frequently voice disagreement with traditional magisterial teaching, particularly on issues pertaining to sexual morality, they still look for ready-made answers to the moral complexities of our day. Many have come to expect of moral theology something it cannot deliver – unchanging timeless truths.

Thus it seems to be crucial to begin to unravel this ambiguity. Clearly, education for responsibility and a recognition of the complexities of all moral issues is essential if we are to respond adequately to this situation. In a climate of growing secularism no Church can depend on legislation to enforce its views on morality. Confidence in its adherents to live according to its values will only be assured if its members are educated for responsibility.

Talk about an ethic of responsibility leads one naturally to the faculty of conscience which has been central to moral discourse through the centuries. In the face of the extension of the scope of authoritative teaching on moral matters[1] and of what Yves Congar termed a creeping infallibilism in magisterial teaching[2] it is essential that we recover the legitimate centrality of the individual conscience in the ecclesial context. To this end it is helpful to explore, however briefly, the various elements in the traditional understanding of conscience in addition to more recent developments which are due mainly to the personalist theology endorsed in the documents of Vatican II, especially the Constitution on the Church in the Modern World, *Gaudium et Spes*.

Historical Dimensions

> When Gentiles who have not the law do by nature what the law required, they are a law to themselves, even though they do not have the law. They show that what the law requires is written on their hearts, while their conscience also bears witness and their conflicting thoughts accuse or perhaps excuse.

Romans 2:14ff is one of the numerous New Testament texts which point to an acknowledgement of the role of conscience in the moral life. The letters to the Corinthians also attend to the idea of conscience with an explicit reference to its role in conflict situations (1 Cor 8:10). The dramatists of Greece were also aware of the potential conflicts between the law and the individual's conscience. Sophocles' *Antigone* is one such play. Commanded not to bury the body of her dead brother, Antigone explicitly affirms her obligation to do what she considers to be right regardless of the law of Creon. She tells Creon: 'I did not think your edicts strong enough/to overrule the unwritten unalterable laws/of God and heaven, you being only a man.'[3]

In its theological development, conscience has been presented in both antecedent and consequent forms. In its antecedent form it has referred to the process of deciding to follow a particular course of action. In this sense, conscience is often understood as a guide or a directive agent: people say, 'My conscience tells me that this is what I should do in this situation'. It comes into operation prior to the particular action; it has a legislative role. Equally prevalent in theological literature is the notion of consequent conscience, the process of reviewing an act and pronouncing judgment as to its moral goodness.

Not even a cursory glance at the history of conscience in ethical discourse can afford to ignore the figure of Thomas Aquinas. Although much can be drawn from his teaching, in particular in relation to the primacy of conscience, I will confine my remarks to how he understood the faculty itself. Aquinas distinguished two elements. There is, first, *synderesis*, a habit belonging not to the will but to practical reason through which one acquires knowledge of primary moral principles. *Conscientia*, on the other hand, is a judgment of the practical intellect, the process of applying these moral principles to particular actions. For Aquinas, then, conscience includes both the innate grasp of the distinction between good and evil and the process of making practical judgments in specific situations.

Psychological theory has also been important in refining the Christian notion of conscience. Thus it needs to be addressed in any attempt to unravel some of the strands which go to make up 'conscience'. Theological reflection frequently contrasts conscience with the 'super-ego'. A Freudian term, super-ego refers to 'the ego of another superimposed on our own to serve as an internal censor or to regulate our conduct by using guilt as its powerful weapon'.[4] Super-ego and conscience differ in significant ways. Super-ego commands one to act to gain approval, is introverted, static i.e. merely repeating a prior command, oriented towards authority. Conscience, in contrast, 'responds to the invitation to love', is extroverted, dynamic, oriented towards value rather than towards authority.[5] It remains a task for adults to continue to move away from a morality based in the responses of the super-ego towards one which is rooted in the dynamism and creativity of conscience.

Enter Vatican II

The understanding of conscience in Scripture and tradition remains the context within which we locate our contemporary discussion. Insights from psychology are also important. However, one of the most significant developments to contribute to the re-emergence of conscience as a key category in moral reflection was the shift to a person-centred moral theology, advanced by the Second Vatican Council.

In its discussion on Christian marriage *Gaudium et Spes* suggested that spouses must determine the moral character of their activity according to 'objective' standards. 'These [are] based on the nature of the human person and of human acts ...' (n. 51). Moral theology is encouraged to move from speaking of the human act in isolation to considering it as a natural reflection of the kind of person one is and one will become. The moral subject becomes the focus of ethical discourse.

A moral theology which has its basis in human personhood differs substantially from one rooted in human nature. Instead of dealing with the human subject as an ahistorical, transcultural being, there is a recognition of the particularity and indeed the complexity of each subject. Kevin Kelly, summarising the work of moral theologians in the past thirty years, suggests that one consider the moral agent as 'a subject, part of the material world, inter-relational with other persons, an interdependent social being, historical, equal but unique, called to know and worship God'.[6]

The shift in moral theology is evident, then, in two arenas. Firstly, there is a move away from considering the morality of acts in isolation. In addition, the language of abstract human nature no longer predominates. Instead, *Gaudium et Spes* confirms the human person, integrally and adequately considered, as the source of moral discernment and action. Although there has been a reluctance to implement the practical conclusions yielded by such a significant shift in foundations, the traditional preoccupation with established norms and principles has indeed been replaced with an emphasis on the formation and education of conscience.

Conscience is located at the heart of Christian morality, requiring of the moral subject adherence to its demands.

> In the depths of their consciences, human persons detect a law which they do not impose on themselves but which holds them to obedience, always summoning them to love good and avoid evil ... For deep in the human heart there is a law written by God. To obey it is the very dignity of the person; according to it one will be judged ... Conscience is the most secret core and sanctuary of the person. There one is alone with God whose voice re-echoes in the soul's depths. (*Gaudium et Spes*, 16)

In an effort to present a holistic vision of conscience, Bernard Häring and others have been involved in reintegrating the dual notions of *synderesis* and *conscientia*, with modifications. Häring speaks of conscience as both the inborn disposition of the will, inclining it to do good and avoid evil through the apprehension of the first moral principles and the judgment of the practical intellect in applying these moral principles to particular actions.[7]

Conscience in common parlance tends to refer to more than practical judgment. It also involves the question of what it means to be human. Conscience refers to the inherent capacity of persons to know and do good. It encompasses the intellectual, emotional and volitional capacities of the person. The integrated self is the valuing subject and as such is the context of all moral choice and action. In his sketch of conscience John Macquarrie distinguished three elements, the most basic of which is conscience as a fundamental mode of self-awareness. This self-awareness, he suggests, discloses the 'gap between our actual selves and that image of our selves that we already have in virtue of the natural inclination towards the fulfilment of man's [sic] end'.[8] Conscience, for Macquarrie, is the inalienable core of the person; it is what makes one human and impels one to become more human. It refers to the summons, the invitation to authentic personhood revealed in the inclination and desire to do the good.

Conscience and Community

Yes, to be human is to be an autonomous centre of discernment and action. However, there is also a relational character of all our lives, and it is only as an historical, embodied, relational subject that one comes to know and choose the good. In this context one can speak of conscience as consciousness of the other[9] and indeed of reciprocity of consciences.[10] Affirming this reciprocity as a key concept in moral theology, Häring suggests:

> I discover that dignity and strength of my own conscience through a profound respect for the

conscience of my neighbour, and indeed for the conscience of every other human being. A genuine reciprocity of consciences is founded on freedom – freedom to love, freedom to listen to each other, freedom to help one another discover the innermost resources of truth, goodness and justice.

Our general sense of value is not acquired in a vacuum but is a reflection of our religious imagination. Conscience as invitation is both an individual and a community event. The Christian narrative provides the world-view through which we interpret and give meaning to our lives. Much has been written on the significance of the Christian story in the moral lives of Christians. Stanley Hauerwas, for example,[11] speaks of the moral self as formed by the Christian narrative. The Christian community is a 'story-formed community'. This community, shaped by the memory of the life and death of Jesus of Nazareth, is the context within which Christians learn to know the good. The community is challenged to be both an interpreter and a vessel of the Christian narrative.

It strikes me as important to note, however, that in its journey to become an embodiment of the Christian vision the Church often falls short. One example is the way in which women's insights have not been heard in formulating official moral teaching. To embody the Christian vision remains a task rather than an accomplishment, not just for the individual but also for the community on its pilgrim way.

Conscience and Choice

In an attempt to live in fidelity to one's vision one is led naturally to conscience as the concrete judgment of what one must do in a particular context. How one chooses is intimately connected to one's ability to discern and evaluate in the midst of moral confusion. Oftentimes, the practical judgment concerning what is right in a particular context will not be clear. Yet with close attention to the situation, and by asking discerning questions, a person learns to have confidence in one's judgment of conscience. Daniel Maguire introduces some 'reality-revealing questions' which enable one to test one's vision and judgment. They are: 'What? Who? When? Why? How? What if? What else?'[12] These questions remind us of the complexity of moral choosing. The intention of the person acting, the motivation, the circumstances in which s/he finds her/himself and the consequences, immediate and long-term – all these impinge on the options available and are relevant to the appraisal of the action.

But what of the status of the individual choice? It appears from the Pauline text and that of *Gaudium et Spes* that choice according to conscience is inviolable, that one is obliged to act always in accordance with the dictates of one's conscience. Indeed the doctrine of the primacy of conscience has been endorsed throughout the Christian tradition. It is particularly associated with Aquinas who recognised that, although a judgment may be erroneous, even an erroneous conscience obliges. 'Every conscience, whether it is right or wrong, whether it concerns things evil in themselves or things morally indifferent, obliges us to act in such a way that one who acts against conscience sins.' (Quodlibet 3, 27)

In the background to such an assertion is, of course, the confidence that reason binds us to seek the moral truth and that 'habitual knowledge of the primary moral principles' inclines us towards what is good. To insist on the primacy of conscience, then, is not an argument for moral relativism. Rather it proceeds from a basic confidence in the goodness of humanity and the capacity and desire to choose the good.

As has already been noted, one's conscience is formed primarily in community – secular and ecclesial. It is, clearly, part of the tradition accepted by believers that the Church, through its pastors, has a duty to teach moral truth to its members, and that Church members have a serious obligation to respect that teaching in forming their consciences. But the Church's role in the apprehension and transmission of value is not as clear-cut as it is sometimes made to seem. Official teaching sets out to formulate principles of general application; and whenever new questions arise (or old questions present themselves in a new context) it may take time before it becomes clear – from experience as much as from official teaching – where the truth lies.

That's why informing one's conscience is not simply a process of uncritically aligning oneself with views expressed by the magisterium. Indeed, one must resist any suggestion that an informed conscience is *always and necessarily* one which is in agreement with an official position. It is accepted that choices made in accordance with an informed and educated conscience can lead to conflict with established values and practices – either secular or ecclesial. Such conflict must, of necessity, be addressed in this discussion.

Conscience and Dissent

There is increasing confusion over the status of the individual dissenter in the Roman Catholic Church. The memory of the Curran case and that of Leonardo Boff has left an indelible mark on the community. The redefinition of the scope of magisterial teaching embodied in the 1989 Profession of Faith and Oath of Fidelity has provoked widespread reaction. While such texts as the Cologne Declaration have been primarily concerned with the role of the theologian in the ecclesial context, the question of legitimate dissent is of interest to all members of the Roman Catholic Church.

A comprehensive consideration of the question would distinguish between infallible teaching, definitive declarations, and non-definitive teaching. I will confine my remarks to the latter since such is the status of most moral teaching. *Obsequium religiosum* is the term most commonly used to describe the appropriate response to non-definitive teaching. The term was used in the Vatican II Constitution on the Church (n. 25) and there have been many disputes as to its meaning. The late Bishop B.C. Butler, O.S.B. aruged that the term meant 'due respect' and held that 'obedience' was too strong a translation.[13]

In coming to this view he cited an article in *L'Osservatore Romano* by a French Jesuit who was believed to have played a part in the drafting of *Humanae Vitae*. The *Osservatore* author pointed out that it was quite wrong to think that the Church in its official teaching expects the faithful to be like photographic film passively reproducing an image imposed on them. The article went on: 'In spite of all appearances to the contrary, it is not the intention of the encyclical to abolish ... legitimate liberty of conscience but only to enlighten consciences and so to help them to be more truly themselves.'

Ladislas Örsy argues that *obsequium religiosum* 'is not, and cannot be, a surrender to God speaking; it is a response to the Church searching'.[14] Such a statement highlights something often forgotten in the frequent disputes over dissent: particularly in moral matters, the entire Church, including the magisterium, is engaged in a search for truth. In answer to the question, '[S]hould we expect the same level of clarity, universality, and evidential force in moral questions as in matters of faith?' William Spohn reminds us of Aristotle's warning that one should not expect 'more certitude from a discipline than its subject matter can afford'.[15] Given the complexities of concrete moral norms and principles, we do well to heed these words.

Individuals have found themselves in conflict with what is taught by the magisterium. While respectful of the teaching office, many in conscience choose contrary to what is taught. It is important, I believe, that theologians affirm that people's experience of living with such conflict can be an important source of moral insight, even when the people themselves may not be acquainted with the finer points of moral theology.

While Richard McCormick's discussion of the search for truth in a Catholic context is focused on theologians, many of the points he makes are also relevant to the individual believer. He highlights the limits of the teaching competence of the magisterium, the importance of dialogue with other disciplines, and the essential contribution of 'those whose faith is involved'.[16] Although many of the points McCormick makes may need to be modified to take account of the 'non-specialist', the same respect is due to both theologian and 'lay member' alike.

A Church which acknowledges the complexities of all moral decision-making and which has faith in the virtue and values of its members will resist calling for external conformity in place of responsible choosing. Most especially in times of transition it is vital to reaffirm the dignity and primacy of the individual's conscience. Informed and confident moral subjects who are capable of discerning what is demanded by the Christian narrative ought to be welcomed rather than silenced. Only then will respectful mutuality characterise intra-ecclesial relationships.

Notes

1   W. Spohn, 'Notes on Moral Theology: 1992', *Theological Studies*, Vol. 54 (1993), p. 95.

2   Cited in Richard McCormick, 'The Search for Truth in a Catholic Context' in Hamel and Himes (eds) *Introduction to Christian Ethics: a Reader* (New York: Paulist Press, 1989), p. 375.

3   Sophocles, *Antigone*, line 452 (Harmondsworth: Penguin 1947). Usually taken as indicating a belief in the natural law, these lines also imply the recognition of what we call conscience.

4   Richard Gula, *Reason Informed by Faith* (New York: Paulist Press, 1989), p. 124.

5   John Glaser, 'Conscience and Superego: A Key Distinction' in Nelson (ed.) *Conscience: Theological and Psychological Perspectives* (New York: Newman Press), 1973, pp. 167–188.

6   Kevin Kelly, 'New Directions' in *Moral Theology: The Challenge of Being Human* (London: Geoffrey Chapman), 1992, p. 30.

7   Bernard Häring, 'Conscience: The Sanctuary of Creative Fidelity and Liberty' in Hamel and Himes, op. cit., pp. 225–280.

8   John MacQuarrie, *Three Issues in Ethics* (London: SCM Press, 1970), p. 113.

9   For an excellent discussion of the failure of conscience as consciousness of the other in an Irish context, see Terence McCaughey, *Memory and Redemption* (Dublin: Gill and Macmillan, 1993); Chapter 9. See also *Doctrine & Life*, March 1993.

10 Bernard Häring in *History and Conscience, Studies in Honour of Seán O'Riodan*, Gallagher and McConvery (eds) (Dublin: Gill & Macmillan, 1989), pp. 60–72. The quotation which follows is at p. 64.

11 Stanley Hauerwas, *A Community of Character* (Notre Dame: University of Notre Press, 1981). Also *Vision and Virtue* (Notre Dame: Fides Publishers nc., 1974).

12 Gula's description in Chapter 5 of *The Moral Choice* (Minnesota: Winston Press, 1978).

13 'Infallible: Authenticum: Assensus: Obsequium: Christian Teaching Authority and the Christian's Response' in *Doctrine & Life*, February 1981, pp. 77–89.

14 See Hamel and Himes, op. cit., p. 334.

15 Art. cit., p. 106, referring to Nicomachean Ethics, 1.3:1-4.

16 McCormick, op. cit.

JUSTIFYING MORAL
POSITIONS

—— Vincent MacNamara ——

In an earlier article[1] I said that the Christian community cannot simply home in on answers to moral problems. The questions may then be asked: how does it do its morality; how does it know that certain things are right or wrong? Or, to put the matter in what may be a more important form: can it help its people to understand why it proposes certain positions to them? The questions can be pushed back a little, but not very successfully. I mean that one may simply appeal to tradition, saying that we have always held such positions and that it would be foolish to depart from them. There is a wisdom in this, but it is not an adequate answer. It will still be asked: how did the community arrive at them in the first place; are we not as competent to consider the same questions; what of the new problems of today?

As a community we do have a great number of positions about morality. Do not steal, or kill, or commit adultery or abortion, or injure another, or engage in pre-marital sex, or break promises, or slander another, or divorce your spouse. It would be wrong to think of the task of the community as simply that of churning out statements of this kind: we have already said something about its task as educator and moulder of moral attitudes. Indeed, it is important that it should not convey the impression that morality can be encompassed by such statements. Even if we had hundreds of them, they would not absolve the individual from the call to grapple with his/her very personal situation, to assess its particularity and to respond to it as fully and as responsibly as possible. They would not substitute for the heart-searching and the sensitivity to persons and situations that conscience-decision requires. But we do have such moral positions. They do play an important part in the community. They represent some kind of framework of morality. They are the features that give rise, very often, to argument about morality.

Today, it has become more important than ever that we examine such positions. Nobody needs reminding that people are daily less inclined to accept directives without explanation. They have learned to question established teaching in many areas of life, to reject some of the old answers, and to expect new insights. They likewise question moral positions. So, the community must examine how it engages in the business of morality. A failure to produce reasons leads to the suspicion that moral positions cannot be justified. A fear that we cannot justify them leads to a defensiveness, that can be mistaken for arrogance or lack of understanding, and that destroys the possibility of dialogue or real education.

I'm sure that Roman Catholic moral theology today presents a picture of some disarray, in comparison with the solidity of a few decades ago. This is so, not only on particular questions, but in its general methodology. The confusion was occasioned, in part, by the breakdown of the traditional scheme of moral theology, in favour of a biblical morality, in the years before Vatican II. This was a highly-important development. But it had the effect of obscuring the whole issue of moral theory. Nobody was clear any longer just how theology purported to arrive at its moral positions. There was a variety of ideas vaguely affecting the climate: the law of Christ, the law of the Spirit, the following of Christ, the sacraments as a basis of moral life, Christ the norm of morality. But no one of them could provide the structural steel that would support a moral theory.

Parallel to this, and independently of it, there took place, within Roman Catholic theology, a re-examination of the natural law theory as it appeared in the moral manual. Everybody knows that holes were picked in the manual treatment. (There is no need to continue the bull baiting here. But it is important to note that it was not just particular conclusions of the theory that were questioned, i.e. why you said that X was wrong, but the theory itself, i.e. why you said that anything was wrong.) It was inevitable that questions about unchanging and universal principles, on which the theory battened, would be raised. The net result, especially for people trained in the older tradition, has been the uncomfortable feeling that that whole house of cards has collapsed. It hasn't. The re-examination was a necessary and healthy exercise. It can only be to the advantage of the Church to be aware of the strength and weaknesses of its positions. Perhaps it was oversimplifying the business of morality, expecting too much of its moral discourse and moral argument. Morality is a very gnarled and knotted area of life. The Church did not make it: she must accept it as it is. It is unlikely that Catholic moral theology will ever again present the unified front of the manuals; that will be matter for regret or satisfaction, depending on your point of view. But it is well to remember that the version of natural law offered by the manual was only one version of a many-skeined tradition. There are theologians today who depart from the manual theory but who consider themselves to be in the genuine natural law tradition.

I do not try, in this article, to elaborate a full-blown moral theory. But I want to do some of the preliminary sketching and to point up some of the problems that surround the business of doing morals. So much depends on how one approaches the problem. I have been suggesting that we should see the moral positions, which we advocate, not as something handed down on Sinai, or anywhere else, but as the wisdom of the community, its response over time to the problem of how man is to live his life. I have said that we do not search for an answer to this question in a vacuum, but within the Judaeo-Christian tradition. This provides us with certain significant key-images of man and reality, which will shape our thinking. One can see something of the history of this search both within and without the Christian community: one has only to think of the development of ideas on such things as slavery, the position of women, children at work, freedom of conscience, capital punishment (or any punishment, for that matter). It can be a liberating thing to realise that what we are dealing with is not some untouchable code but a morality fashioned by people like ourselves, people in some ways less enlightened than ourselves. Aquinas tells us that the difference between man and the rest of creation, in God's plan, is that man is to provide for himself and discover his own law. In every age, it is our responsibility not only to live morally, but to decide what living morally means. It is through the demands of our intelligence that we know God's will: our moral positions are God's will to the extent that they are rational. But none of us is pure reason walking around. It is a sinful lot who do the reasoning, so much so that sometimes we can't even see the questions, never mind the answers. So, it is God-fearing not to be smug about our own answers or about the answers handed down to us, but to be ever searching and questioning.

It is only one who sees the business of the discovery of morality as above and beyond and apart from us and as, once and for all, settled somewhere who will opt out of the questioning. Perhaps one who considers that, as Christians, we have some clear and unmistakable source of moral information, such as the

Bible, where moral problems are solved for all time. But we have seen that such an approach will not do. The coming of Christ did not solve the moral problems of the world. Peter and Paul and their successors in the Church still had to struggle and wonder about answers to moral questions. They had, indeed, the kind of enlightenment and encouragement from their faith which we have already considered. They had the tradition about Jesus, his sayings and doings. But it did not absolve them from the task of searching. And they were often glad to find help in Plato, or Aristotle, or Cicero.

So, the quest for the truly human and Christian life goes on in the community. It must not be done out of relation to the tradition, but in continuity with it, in the realisation that we are, in our day, trying to do what former ages were trying to do in theirs. It is a quest in which all have a part to play; insight about decent living is not the monopoly of any one group. But there will be some who will have lived experience of particular areas of life to throw into the kitty of knowledge. I suppose it would be too much to hope that such ongoing analysis of something so close to the bone as morality could be realised without tension. There will be some in the community who will rely heavily on traditional positions and who will trust that truth and wisdom are more likely to be found in them, until the opposite is proven absolutely. There are others for whom the past is a valid but partial and time-conditioned insight. These will point, rather, to the historical nature of all human knowledge. If man's understanding of himself has been growing, they will see no reason why his moral discovery should not be ongoing. They will do this as a matter of course. Both sides will feel an obligation to the truth and to God to pursue their line of thought.

The tension between these two elements can be fruitful for the community, if it can be conducted with tolerance. It is important for the community that its inherited wisdom should not be carelessly frittered away. It is equally important for it that it should not be immobilised in its past. But it would be a mistake for anyone to feel that everything is up for grabs and that we have no solid ground under our feet anymore. Perhaps, one can take comfort in such documents as the UN Declaration on Human Rights or the European Convention on Rights. They bear witness to the conviction of many communities that there is a right way of living. Most of us are prepared to trust that conviction. We may not be able to found it or theorise about it or work out its implications. We may disagree with others both about the basis and the details of it. But our experience – perhaps a particularly sharp experience in some areas of life – convinces us that it does matter how one lives and that it cannot be an arbitrary matter. Life is not a matter of brute facts. However you prove it or explain it or produce a theory about it, six million Jews ought not to be killed. Men ought not to be tortured or forced to act against their conscience. Children ought not to be starved or deceived or exploited. And these judgments, we are convinced, are not just a matter of taste.

This represents our unreflective experience. If pressed further to give some account of why we regard certain kinds of activity as good or bad, we might find ourselves struggling with concepts like, 'the flourishing of man', 'the needs of man', 'the dignity of man', 'what is fitting to man'. I think we would be trying to articulate our experience of the worth of the human person – ourselves and others – of the good sense of his flourishing and the senselessness of his diminishment. We would, I imagine, be trying to say that we only reach our own fulfilment, we are only at peace with ourselves, when we live in a way that accepts and responds to the worth of others. Otherwise, we find, our own lives are diminished. So that, in fact, our attitude to the other's flourishing determines our own. It is not an empty recognition: we have at least a partially formed understanding of what such acceptance and response might involve. There are goods in life which naturally commend themselves to all of us, which we consider to be closely connected with the business of being human, which we know to be useful or important or crucial because of how we experience ourselves as human beings.

So, for example, it is important to all of us that we know the truth and not live in error, that we have self-esteem, that we be accepted into and participate in social life, that we have enough to eat, that we be virtuous, that we be not impaired mentally or emotionally, that we be able to relate to others. It is foundational to this that we have life and health and freedom. And it appears necessary to it that we enter into relations, which give rise to a special bond (trust, promise, commitment, parenthood, etc.) This is the stuff of life. The Christian will share all this with others, but he/she will see knowledge of God and friendship with Him as the supreme values. It is out of this kind of lived experience that we have some perception of how to shape our lives. If the intelligent life is not one which preserves such values, it is very hard to know what it could be.

So, we feel justified in saying that morality lies in the direction of respect for the other, of fairness and impartiality. It lies in the direction of respect for life, care for its handing on, nurture of the young and defenceless. It is in the direction of seeking the truth, allowing others to seek it, not denying it to them. It is in the direction of ensuring freedom. It is in the direction of trust and fidelity. It is in the direction of allowing others to mature, of healing and making whole. These are the convictions of most of us in our saner moments. The statements are very general of course. But, they are not empty: they indicate the general direction of the good life. We know in a rough way what kind of behaviour is being commended or ruled out. We find, in fact, that appeals at this level play an important part in life: they have a curiously evocative power. Calls for justice, fraternity, equality, awaken a spontaneous response in us. They are the kind of cry that arouses moral indignation and starts revolutions. But statements at this level do not specify exactly the piece of behaviour that qualifies as good or bad. One might well ask us what we mean by justice, or fairness or concern for freedom. One might ask us to declare the precise piece of behaviour that would count as not caring for justice, or fairness, or freedom.

Some people refer to statements at this level of moral discourse as *prima facie* rules, other refer to them as moral values, others as principles. One feels relatively confident about statements of this kind and disagreement about them is less likely than about statements of a more determinate kind. (Incidentally, it is well to note that people often agree about substantive moral positions, although they disagree in elaborating a theory about them.) It is, I suppose, possible to imagine a situation in which a community would propose to its members only this general level of principle. But, in fact, the Church, both in its official teaching and in its general theology, has been accustomed to declare the rightness and wrongness of actions in a much more detailed manner: it has been accustomed to propose what some refer to as moral rules. It is at this level that most of the problems arise. Rules are typically negative: what is distinctive about them is that they *are* prepared to name precisely what is good or bad living. 'Promise-breaking is wrong', 'Adultery is wrong', 'Pre-marital sex is wrong', if taken in their obvious sense, are typical forms. (They are not taken in their normal and obvious form by some, but I cannot go into that here.) It is quite clear here what piece of behaviour is intended.

What this means is that our moral thinking and language operate at different levels of generality or particularity. The justification of a moral rule is that it is concretizing a value or principle in a piece of behaviour. It is saying that this behaviour embodies an attack on a value and is, therefore, to be avoided. I am not saying that we always go through or need to go through an elaborate argumentation. But, sometimes, we do. We cannot just jump to conclusions. We may need a lot of information: some of it may be provided by the behavioural sciences, for example. Take a problem like the right to work, which I found myself discussing recently in a group. I presume we were asking whether the community has an obligation to organise itself so that as many as possible would have work – or something like that. Suggestions about mere support or the need for creative outlet were ruled out early on – they could be provided for otherwise. The main suggestions were that a man needs to feel independent, that he suffers a loss of self-respect and a lowering of morale, that he experiences a sense of frustration and humiliation, if he has to draw the dole continually – in short, that he needs to feel that he is honestly earning his living by his work. We seemed to be starting out from the respect due to others and to be asking just what that involved or when it was lacking. But there was a question: is it true that this is the case, that man does feel humiliated and debased and alienated in such circumstances? That requires finding out. It means asking people who know, perhaps such as industrial psychologists. And, if one were to push the question further, it could be asked if one's conclusions here were valid only for a particular time and culture, because of the role which work happens to play now in our society.

The main point of this article is to say that, when we are asked to justify moral positions – as we will be – there is no need to panic but every reason for engaging in dialogue. People may, indeed, disagree with us about details. But we can at least hope to give a good account of ourselves and to show that our morality is really our interest to make sense of ourselves and to find what protects and enhances human life, as it has been given to us. Here, of course, I have tried only to sketch in the outline. Most people will realise that there is a whole host of questions that can be asked at this point. That would demand development and refinement of what has been said but not, I think, major reversal. Such questions I must leave, but I want to come back to moral argumentation.

It can be seen that, if you are proposing a position about morality, you cannot expect to prove your point as you would in the natural sciences. If you think you can, you are heading for frustration. Educators and preachers sometimes feel that there is something wrong with them if they cannot prove and copper-fasten a point of moral argument. But moral argument doesn't work like that. It admits of only a limited type of 'demonstration'. It is filtered through a sensitivity to the demands of the human spirit and through an appeal to the experience of men and to the demands, even, of a particular culture. But this is difficult. It calls for imagination and vision. We have considered earlier how a person may become more or less open or closed to this kind of discrimination of what is good for man – partly through his past actions, but also through environment, heredity, culture. This is not to say that a community should only demand from its members what they can 'see'. But, fully moral activity involves 'seeing'.

Another, and related, point. I have been using words such as 'human' and 'humanising' rather cavalierly, as if their meaning were quite clear. It isn't. The question of the 'human' is one of the most anxiously debated in moral theology. Is it humanly desirable (does it accord with our perception of what it is to live humanly) to engage in genetic manipulation, and to what extent? What of IVF, in the case of a childless couple? What of the determination of the sex of children? Is it good that the psychological processes of criminals by 'interfered' with, and to what extent? What of capital punishment? How is one to balance the treatment of a terminally ill patient against his dignified dying? These are random examples and the questions are just raised to make a point. Heaven only knows what kind of manipulation of humankind's life may be possible in future: what will count as human and what as inhuman? It is important to remember that they are questions for all of us – not just for doctors or geneticists or criminologists – for our understanding of ourselves and our perception of what is good or fitting for our lives.

⬤ Two more points. I think we have to learn to live with the fact that we don't have and don't have to have all the answers. Some find that difficult to take. But we are ignorant of so much. We have had to muddle through with only the most rudimentary notions in psychology, for example – without knowing important things about the springs of our thoughts and actions. We realise now that even our prized scientific theories are tentative. There are more important areas in which we are ignorant. We know so little about God. If anything, we are less ready to make statements about Him than we were yesteryear. We seem to have more problems about Christ than we had a few years ago. We know hardly anything about the Last Things. And, yet, we survive and keep searching. We have to live with uncertainty, with our finiteness. Humankind, fortunately, is much more mysterious and profound than a machine and a certain modesty is not out of place in making pronouncements about it. There can be no penny-in-the-slot answers.

One is often asked in despair: 'Who, then, is to say what is right?' The implication may be that there must be some slot somewhere, where we can put our pennies. But there isn't. It may be that a Christian will have, on some particular issue, an assurance from his Church that the answer is so-and-so. That is a special case. It may also be that, short of this, there is a firm tradition: one who would not take account of it would be a fool or a knave. But, the overall answer is that there is nowhere to go, except to ourselves. As I said at the outset, we have to try to figure it out the best we can. All we can do is put our Christian heads together. We can only hope, when we seek to solve some moral problem, as individuals or a community, that we are doing it right, that we are as careful as possible to try to understand ourselves, and that, as far as possible, we try to rid ourselves of what would prevent true insight – prejudice, passion, bias. We can only keep hoping and praying that rationality will break through. Aristotle's advice to those who wanted to know how one should live was that they go to the good man. In the practicalities of life, his advice is not the vicious circle it might appear to be. We can only hope that we shall continue to have such women and men in our communities and churches.

Finally, we didn't come down in the last shower. Our people have been at this sort of thing for a long time. Even if we don't have all the answers – no system could provide for the particularities of our personal situations – we do absorb from our faith points of view that mark parameters and guidelines of thought. For example, if one takes faith seriously, it is not possible to think of human flourishing or to weigh values solely in terms of this world's horizons. It is not possible to be unaware of the value of human life or of the dignity of the least among us. It is put up to us to reflect on God's dealings with humankind since the beginning, and on Christ's life on earth and to draw conclusions for our own lives. Earlier, I said something of the way in which these perspectives should enlighten and refine our efforts to discover what it means to be man.[2] But they don't absolve us from thinking and trying to justify our positions. They do form the world-view in which all our thinking is done. A last thought might be that it is also done in a tradition which has some awareness of the sin and blindness of man and which knows the need to pray for light and guidance.

Notes
1   See Chapter 3.
2   See Chapter 4.

MORAL CHARACTER

—— Bill Cosgrave ——

In discussing moral character we will be discussing a rather neglected topic in contemporary Catholic moral reflection. It will be helpful to begin with a look at the past, which will give us some insight into why our subject was so little talked about in earlier times. Then we can move on to look at contemporary moral thinking in the Church, and that will provide us with the context in which to elaborate the basic aspects and dimensions of moral character. We will, then, see more clearly why there is today a renewed interest in this important element of our Christian moral lives.

The legal understanding or model of the moral life was very act-centred, i.e. it concerned itself largely with the individual moral actions that a person performed or could perform. Moral living seemed to consist of doing as many good acts as possible and avoiding wrong acts. There was little focus on the person doing the acts and what effect these actions were having on her/him and on her/his growth or decline in goodness and virtue. Hence, there was little concern for moral character or the virtues that constitute its various dimensions.

Pre-Vatican II moral theology and spirituality would speak of themselves as elaborating an ethic of virtue, but in practice that meant only that the virtues gave rise to further obligations to do more specific acts. This was still an act-centred conception of the virtues. Here we see another reason why the legal model of the Christian moral life has been considered inadequate and has in recent decades been replaced by the relational model. To this we now turn.

This understanding of the Christian moral life focuses primarily on the person-in-relationship-and-in-community and, therefore, on the moral subject and her/his growth or decline in goodness and virtue. Specific actions retain their importance but only in the context of the person and what is happening to her/him morally speaking. In this model an essential pre-requisite is an adequate understanding of the human person. We will assume this anthropology here and devote our attention to the person as a moral subject, to her/his moral character and its formation and growth (or lack of it) and the practical implications of this for our moral lives as Christians.

What is Moral Character?
We know from experience that certain people are generally consistent in the way they react to situations. We can rely on them to make a certain type of response in most circumstances. They are predictable and seem to have certain stable characteristics. This predictability and reliability seems to come from these people's commitment to particular values and from their maintaining certain attitudes and intentions. People often refer to this predictability and stability as the person's character. That is the word we will use here. Others call it integrity.[1]

This character, which manifests itself through one's actions and is clearly a moral reality, refers to who one is as a human being. It is one's moral identity as a person, one's moral self. My moral character is who I have made myself over my lifetime so far, particularly as a result of my moral choices. Each person's moral character consists of a very specific and personal configuration or arrangement of virtues and vices, affections, intentions, dispositions, beliefs, values and priorities. One's character gives one a particular direction or orientation in and to life, so that one acts in a consistent way, either doing good or doing evil. The character one has built represents the characteristic way one has of determining what is appropriate for one to do in any particular situation. Everyone's character is unique and no one type of character is normative.[2]

The issue of character is, then, the basic issue for each person in her/his moral life. This is confirmed by experience where we discover that, along with the call to do good deeds, we also experience the call, from the depth of our being as persons and ultimately from God, to become good persons. Hence, our moral lives must be concerned above all with the kind of persons we are, are becoming and ought to become. It will be important for us, then, to reflect well on this question of our moral character, so as to understand it and its central importance better and do all possible to build that character more fully.

Building Moral Character

As human beings we all have important duties or calls to do good in various ways and forms. At the same time, as was noted just now, we can discern in our deeper selves a call or invitation to become a good person, to build our moral self or character so taut we become the best human being we can become. Hence, while it is important to be kind, just and generous, it is more important for each individual to become a good person, to build one's character to its highest level. As Christians we experience this call as an invitation from Jesus to become the best disciples of Christ we can be, so as to become fully mature with the fullness of Christ (Eph 4:13).

Building one's moral character can only be achieved, of course, through the particular choices and actions one performs. These choices spring from one's goodness of character, and they confirm and strengthen that goodness. Despite this importance that attaches to our particular choices, however, focusing on one's call to character building remains primary and essential. This focus will ensure that we avoid an act-centred moral outlook, get our priorities right and keep in mind the process nature of the journey towards maturity as a human being and a Christian.

The two central points here can be stated immediately. Firstly, our moral choices shape and form our moral character but, secondly, it is also true that our moral character gives rise to and conditions our moral choices. So there is a two-way influence between character and choice. Our choices make us who we are as persons. By acting in certain ways consistently we make ourselves to be certain sorts of persons, either for good or for evil. On the other hand, who we are now as persons powerfully influences and conditions what we choose to do or not do. So, if a person performs many acts of generosity over many years, then he/she will become a generous person; generosity will be an important virtue or quality in his/her moral character. Similarly with a vice–like laziness. The other side of this coin is that one who is a just person will usually act in a just way, while one who is intemperate will usually behave intemperately. Note here that we say 'usually'. Few, if any, people are always generous or lazy or just. Most act in those ways only most of the time. Even the best of people act out of character, as they say, now and again. Evidently, then, there is some good in the worst of us and some bad in the best of us. Obviously too, there can be degrees of goodness and badness in one's character. Some are very good (or bad) indeed, while others are clearly less consistently good (or bad). It even seems the case that some haven't as yet determined a direction in their way of choosing and so let the direction vary from one decision to another.[3]

Our particular moral choices or actions usually have a twofold effect. They have an impact on a specific situation, e.g. I help an injured person or steal someone's money. But these choices also have an impact on me as a moral subject, as their doer. They make me a more or less good person and so they form my character for better or for worse. Thus caring for another person in need makes me a more caring and loving person, while stealing another's property makes me more sinful, less good and loving and so deforms my moral character, and makes it more likely that I will sin again in the future. In the legal model of the moral life these negative effects of one's sinful choices are spoken of as the 'punishments' for sin. But in the relational model they appear as the natural consequences of doing something that is sinful.

Experience indicates that our choices have different degrees of goodness and badness. Some are minor, some are serious. Today the Church is clear that occasionally we can make a very profound choice that will affect our character very significantly. We are capable of what is frequently called a fundamental opinion or basic choice. This is a profound choice for good or evil that can change one's character from being good and loving to being selfish and sinful or vice versa. Such choices will be rare because they are difficult and demand deep knowledge, real commitment of heart and usually a serious issue to evoke them.

In the context, then, of concern for our moral character individual moral choices retain their essential importance. They build up or damage our moral character and so are the means by which we become better or worse persons. Our doing impacts on our being and makes us what we are.

In talking about moral character we have been speaking of it as good and bad or good and evil. We talked of a person's moral goodness or badness. This presents no difficulty in itself. But in our moral discourse we also make use of the terms right and wrong, moral and immoral. Strictly speaking, these refer only to choices or actions, not to persons or their character. Thus goodness and badness pertain to persons and their characters only, whereas rightness and wrongness are attributed only to choices and actions.

This distinction points up the fact that morality is, first of all, applicable to persons and their characters and only secondarily to choices and actions. These latter are moral only in an analogous sense. This is also clear from the fact that only persons can be moral agents and as such are the source of choices and actions. In addition, only persons can construct moral or just communities, and central to such construction is moral character, what the community members are as moral persons. Thus we have convincing reasons for giving the priority to moral character and its formation over particular choices and actions in relation to both individuals and communities.[4]

While this is a more complex and difficult concept to understand than character in relation to an individual person, we can speak of a group or community character in so far as that group or community is based on and held together by its common choices and activities. Thus we may speak of a marriage as a community that has a moral character arising from the couple's choice to marry each other and their subsequent choices that maintain and strengthen (or weaken) their union. In a similar way one may refer to the moral character of a family or neighbourhood or even a society or political community. Thus, to speak of the 'Irish character' does make sense, since we as a nation have in common many values, such as commitment to democracy, the equality of all, the consequent requirement of justice and fairness as well as other values and virtues.[5]

We can speak also of the Church as having a quite definite character. This character arises from and is maintained by the

Church's commitment to and action in support of the Gospel and kingdom values and virtues which Jesus originally preached, exemplified in his life and passed on to his followers. This character of the Church community undoubtedly influences its members but they in turn exercise an influence on it in a variety of ways and to varying degrees. The same holds for society. And, of course, the influence can be positive and negative in both directions in society as well as in the Church.

Formation of Moral Character
We know from experience that our own and other people's characters become what they are and will be at end of life only by a long and complex process of formation, both formal and informal. This usually involves growth and development but also very likely some regression and sin. This formation will be lifelong and so always ongoing, though the most decisive elements of it will probably make their impact in the earlier part of life.

Some nowadays prefer to talk of formation in virtue rather than of character formation, while others treat it all as simply formation of conscience, understood in its deepest sense of the moral subject living by a certain set of values, ideals and principles that ground his/her moral judgments and decisions. These are valid approaches but we will continue to refer to character and what forms it in goodness and virtue. Whatever approach one takes, one's main aim must be that we all become good and virtuous people, morally or humanly mature. This will enable us to actualise our potential for being and doing good or, simply, for being loving persons and doing loving actions. For the Christian this involves formation in loving God and one's neighbour as essential elements in building Christian character and in strengthening the kingdom of God on earth.

Conditioning Factors

The formation of character requires attention to three factors or realities that are internal to the moral subject.

- *Knowledge*: This is not abstract knowledge of ideas or theories but rather evaluative or experiential knowledge of moral values and disvalues, particularly those concerning the appreciation of persons and what is for their welfare against it. Essential here too is knowledge or awareness of oneself, in particular awareness of one's values, attitudes, dispositions, intentions, feelings, needs, weaknesses, blind spots, limitations and level of moral development. This awareness is the cornerstone of moral, spiritual and psychological growth.[6]

- *Freedom*: Formation of character requires true personal freedom in each person, so that we can take fuller responsibility for our choices and for what we have made of ourselves as persons up to now and for our future. The greater our freedom from internal and external obstacles, the greater will be our ability to form ourselves as moral persons in character and in virtue. Theologians today speak, not just of our freedom to choose particular responses or actions, but also of our freedom to choose who and what we will become as persons, whether good or bad. This freedom is called basic freedom and it is exercised in what we have referred to as fundamental options or basic choices. Working to increase this form of freedom will clearly be greatly significant for our character formation.

- *Emotions*: In the past we considered our emotions in a large measure an obstacle to the proper formation of our moral character but today we have a much better and more positive appreciation of their role in our personality and in our moral lives. A person's morality or moral sense has its roots in his/her feelings. From them our morality gets its nourishment and power to shape our character and our choices. This means that the springs of morality are in the heart, especially the basic experience we have of value, in particular the value of persons. Values or goods are appreciated emotionally or affectively as well as intellectually. This affective appreciation has an element of judgment or evaluation in it, thus giving us a preliminary moral assessment of any choice we are contemplating. It is clear, then, that emotion pervades our moral knowledge and has an important contribution to make to our moral choices and our character building. Feelings can guide our perceptions and moral judgments and they give energy to our commitments and our drive to become good persons. In fact, for the person with a good moral character one's feelings can make appropriate moral choices second nature, as it were. This happens because our emotions give us deeper insight into the values we love and facilitate us in judging and choosing wisely and well in their regard.

All this helps explain why the emotionally immature person will very likely have a diminished level of moral maturity or of character formation. An example: bad anger or bad mood control and lack of empathy, giving rise to conflict, damaged relationships and lack of care for others. On the other hand, one with greater emotional maturity will probably achieve a higher level of moral maturity and so of character growth. Hence, she/he will usually do better in controlling anger and 'bad humour', etc. and will generally display greater empathy with others. In consequence, he/she will make better moral choices and advance more in the formation of character in goodness.[7]

It is true that each person forms his/her own character but that does not exclude the fact that we are all influenced in very significant ways by the groups, communities and society we live in at any particular time and, in the case of Christians, by the Church too.

While it is true that people make groups and communities, it is also a fact that in a real sense groups and communities make people. We are deeply moulded by the groups we belong to and usually we internalise the patterns of thinking, communicating and behaving of these groups. We are influenced also by the beliefs, values, virtues and attitudes of the groups of which we are members. In particular we learn to value persons and tend to identify with the ways people treat each other in our communities. Morality is, then, in significant ways socially conditioned or a social product and this impacts very profoundly on our character formation.

The Church as Moral Community

The Church, through its vision of human life with its beliefs, stories, traditions, images and rituals, moral ideals, values, principles and virtues is a powerful shaper of our moral character. Particularly important will be the Bible, the example of Jesus and the life and teaching of the Church itself along with the saints and other outstanding personages of the Christian community. Each one will respond to these influences in her/his own way and thus will make her/his choices and form her/his character in a manner that is uniquely personal.

Ways of Describing Good Moral Character

It will be useful to set out briefly four different ways in which we speak of the good moral character or the person who has grown significantly in moral goodness and virtue. These have been mentioned in passing earlier but a brief reflection on these descriptions of the ideal of goodness will be worthwhile.

- *Being fully human:* A person who has formed a good moral character may be spoken of as well advanced towards being fully human, i.e. to have progressed well along the road to fulfilment as a person and so to have realised substantially one's potential as a human person. Hence, having a good moral character is something that humanises you, makes you a better human being, a more human person. This is a lifelong project, of course, but it is encouraging to realise that moral living is not some burden imposed on us by an outside agent like the State or the Church or God. Rather, it is what our very nature as persons calls for and pushes us to do.

- *Being a loving person:* A person with good moral character is one who loves self, others and God. One is good to the extent that one is loving and that means caring in an unselfish and mature manner in the relationships one has with oneself, other people and God. To put this in other words, being loving involves and requires one to have all the virtues in some real degree, because love expresses itself in and through those virtues.

- *Being a virtuous person:* Another way of speaking of a person with a good moral character is to say that he/she is a virtuous person. To be virtuous is to have acquired those habits, attitudes, affections and beliefs that are called the virtues and to practise them consistently in one's daily life. Doing this makes one a good person because it builds up one's moral character. Today the virtues are getting a lot more attention than they got before Vatican II and the Christian ethic is frequently referred to nowadays as an ethic of virtue. In this context more emphasis is placed on moral character, and it is being restored to the central place it should always have occupied.

- *Being a morally mature person:* This way of speaking of good moral character indicates that the person has grown morally to a level appropriate to his/her stage in life's journey. It points also to the importance of emotional, personal and relational growth and maturity as foundations for moral maturity. Without them one will probably be rendered unable to achieve real maturity at the moral level.

Practical Implications

Putting moral character at the centre of our moral reflections and living will help us to move away from an act-centred understanding of the Christian moral life and enable us to give more attention to our growth as whole persons.

Emphasising moral character helps one to remain aware of the fact that the Christian life is a process of growth (and possibly decline) over time and requires continuing effort and attention. This holds true also of the talk of conversion from sinfulness. So we are always called to deeper conversion and fuller growth in moral character or Christian virtue.

While one may 'get away' with sin and the sense that others may not find out about it, it always does damage to the sinner's moral character by making him/her less loving and more inclined to sin in the future. The opposite happens when one performs a virtuous act. This builds character and makes one a better person.

The more one builds one's moral character, the more one is inclined to do good and avoid sin. So one who has lived a good life for many years need not be anxious about falling into serious sin, especially at the last minute of life. We seldom act out of character. But, since that is possible, there is no room for complacency.

To assist in our growth towards a good moral character we need to respond positively but critically to the influences of the various groups and communities of which we are members. In doing so the Church's teaching will be essential and will provide direction and directions.

To assess oneself morally, or in other words, to examine one's conscience, it will help to focus on particular virtues (and vices) as important dimensions of one's moral character, and also on the quality of one's part in the various relationships one has.

Finally, one cannot attain perfection of character here on earth. Perfection is for heaven only. Hence, we will always be imperfect here below. What we are called to is continuing growth and character building. We can then be confident in the hope that God will bring us to the fulfilment we have desired and for which we have worked throughout our lives.

Notes

1   James M. Gustasfon, *Christian Ethics and the Community* (Philadelphia, USA: Pilgrim Press, 1971), pp. 166–172.
2   Stanley Hauerwas, *Character and the Christian Life: A Study in Theological Ethics* (San Antonio, USA: Trinity University Press, 1975), p. 127.
3   Hauerwas, p. 122.
4   See Russell B. Connors Jnr. and Patrick T. McCormick, *Character Choices and Community – The Three Faces of Christian Ethics* (New York: Paulist Press, 1998), pp. 22–24.
5   Germain Grisez and Russell Shaw, *Fulfilment in Christ – A Summary of Christian Moral Principles* (Notre Dame and London: University of Notre Dame, 1991), pp. 24–5.
6   Richard M. Gula SS, *Moral Discernment* (New York: Paulist Press, 1997), pp. 27–40 at p. 28.
7   See Gula, *Moral Discernment*, pp. 34–9 and 67–91; also Daniel Maguire, *Moral Choice* (Minneapolis, USA: Winston Press, 1979), pp. 71–7, 281–308.

CAN GOODNESS
BE TAUGHT?

—— Pádraig Hogan ——

Some Initial Difficulties

A recurring cautionary voice suggests to me that it is foolhardy, maybe even futile, to tackle the question posed in the title. The question comes to the fore with a new urgency however at times of major social and cultural change, such as we have been experiencing in Ireland in recent years. The moral turbulence associated with such change manifests itself strongly in relations between parents and their children, and often becomes acute in post-primary schools, where adolescent cultures come face-to-face with the more established outlooks of teachers. Teachers of religion particularly find themselves in the midst of such turbulence, and are somehow expected to provide some kind of practical resolution to a question that great numbers of parents and other adults find intractable. Perhaps if more prudent counsel prevailed, one would simply accept the question as unanswerable and leave it aside from the already busy concerns of education. To close the question in this way however is to decline what is particularly worthy of our best efforts to understand. It is to do less than justice to the searching spirit of those Greeks who originally raised the question publicly. Not least, it is to turn a blind eye to the difficulties which the question increasingly places in the path of today's teachers.

Christianity in one form or another has invariably been a central feature of the western cultural heritage. What is not sufficiently acknowledged however is that this may not be so for the future. During the twentieth century the pervasive influences of a secular world order and the dazzling effects of an international communications and entertainments technology altered significantly the major constituents of the western cultural heritage itself. It is not so much that humankind has become averse to all moral influences; rather that any body of moral teaching which is seen to spring primarily from long established authority and tradition is likely nowadays to encounter widescale rejection or indifference, particularly where the sensibilities of the young are concerned.

As early as the late nineteen thirties, this tendency was well described by Martin Buber in his distinguished essay 'The Education of Character'. There Buber wrote: 'But to deny the presence of universal values and norms of absolute validity – that is the conspicuous tendency of our age.'[1] Buber was acutely conscious of the special difficulties confronting moral education in an age of increasing pluralism:

> But as soon as my pupils notice that I want to
> educate their characters I am resisted precisely by
> those who show most signs of genuine
> independent character: they will not let
> themselves be educated, or rather, they do not like
> the idea that somebody wants to educate them.[2]

One of the points that stands out most clearly in my own mind over many years of dealings with student teachers, school principals and post-primary teachers, is the extent to which Buber's observation here has been repeatedly confirmed in the experience of teachers of religion in Irish post-primary schools.

The view is now widespread among teachers of religion in the schools, and widely shared by school principals, that, where the teaching of religion and morality are concerned, one cannot make the same assumptions about an assembly of students in a classroom as one might make about a congregation which has voluntarily assembled in a church. What this expresses, apart from any special difficulties posed by present-day cultural diversities, is the distinction between an educational interest and an evangelical interest, or an institutional interest, in moral or religious tradition. The failure to make this distinction *in schools*, in addition to inviting charges of indoctrination at one level, tends to foredoom the efforts of teachers at another. A practical conclusion to be drawn from these reflections is that a tradition of religious or moral teaching is, properly speaking, introduced into a schooling context on a quite different set of considerations from that on which the same tradition might be engaged by a community of believers or disciples.

An awareness of the significance of this last point seems to underlie the new programmes in religious education that have been introduced in post-primary schools during the last decade. With the advent of these programmes a traditional emphasis on the teaching of religion as a form of faith nurturing has witnessed the rise of a new emphasis on critical exploration; exploration of religious experience, of religious belief systems and of personal religious convictions. The older approaches would largely answer the question posed in our title with an earnest 'yes', and then proceed unproblematically, if often through uphill struggle, on that basis. The newer approaches tend to render problematic, however, just what was most time-honoured and decisive in the older pedagogy. This may well be salutary. But they also tend to remove from centre-stage a critical awareness of the import of the question 'Can goodness be taught?' And this is regrettable. Goodness *can* be learned, *is* continually being learned *and* unlearned, in the everyday experiences of being human in a world shared with others. If we could understand better how teaching, rather than frustrate or take custody of such unforced learning, could turn it to more fruitful purpose, we should have made a significant advance in pursuing our question.

Unearthing a Few Clues

Perhaps the most promising and economical way to find a path to such an advance is to avail ourselves of two very useful insights from the Greeks. The first of these insights we owe to Plato (or more strictly, Socrates) and, simply stated, it tells us that the question 'can goodness be taught?' cannot properly be engaged unless we tackle in a practical setting the question of what goodness is. Of course different religious traditions provide different answers to this question. And in an age when pluralism as a civic virtue is commonly promoted in the countries that are heirs to western civilisation, it is crucial that students become informed of these different answers. But necessary as this is, it is not sufficient. One could be quite informed and devout in one's religious beliefs, and be notably tolerant of other traditions, and yet reveal a notable absence of goodness in one's daily actions; the kind of goodness that makes a practical difference. So pursuing the question of goodness in a practical setting highlights the issue of *ēthos*, as well as the particulars of moral traditions, and brings us to a further insight. This we owe largely to Aristotle (*Nic. Ethics,* Book 2). It can be put as follows. Our moral character is influenced much more by what becomes habitual in our everyday lives than it is by the contents of a programme of moral instruction; more by *ēthos* as an emergent quality than by *ēthos* as a prescribed or enforced quality.

Taking these two insights together, their educational import is far-reaching indeed. What they suggest is a decisive but also very circumspect 'yes' to the question posed in our title. They warn us away from detailed syllabi and from mass-produced textbooks. They urge instead attention to locally achieveable, if initially modest, goals. In specific terms these combined insights call for the building up and maintenance of a shared *ēthos* where practices of exploration and reflection, of listening and deliberation, of discernment and informed choosing, have themselves to become habitual; have effectively become a moral orientation, or disposition. For teachers this represents a prospect which is singularly inviting, but maybe also quite daunting. We shall return to this point in the next part of our enquiry, but first let us consider a possible objection. The objection is that any teaching of morality which departs from a direct instruction in doctrines invites confusion on the part of the learners.

Taking Christianity as our example of a religious tradition, perhaps the most concise, yet effective way of dealing with this objection is to refer it to the teaching approach employed by Jesus, particularly when he addressed those heterogeneous and potentially clamorous groups described in the Gospels as 'multitudes':

> All these things Jesus spoke in parables to the multitudes and *without parables he did not speak to them.*
>
> (Mt 13:34; Mk 4:33-34; emphasis added)

We are probably so familiar with this verse that we fail to be pulled up short by the incisive pedagogical insight in the last phrase: *Only* through parables did Jesus teach the multitudes. With the disciples he took a different and more direct approach (Mk 4:34). The importance of this illustration rests in realising that the distinction between 'multitudes' and 'disciples' is as relevant now as it was then. Accordingly the perceptiveness of Jesus is worthy of our closest attention as teachers. We need only add that the classrooms of today contain 'multitudes' on a scale without precedent.

Conscience and the Claims of Tradition

What happens, however, after the ingenuity of the teacher succeeds in bringing students to listen to the voice of a moral or religious tradition which seeks to address them? Characteristically what happens next is that the students' whetted spiritual sensibilities reveal themselves in continuous and challenging questions. In this regard one of the merits of investigative approaches is that they regularly succeed in arousing interest in moral questions in a way that direct moral instruction repeatedly fails to do. Acts of clarification in moral deliberation however usually involve some exercise of moral *judgment*, even if only tacit judgment, on the part of those involved in working out the clarification. This exercise of judgment moreover necessarily involves the conscience of the individual – either by sharpening it, and thus educating it, or by dulling or seducing it, and thus miseducating it.

A further point needs to be noted here. The crucial involvement of conscience in any educational effort to explore a moral concept or a religious teaching is neglected not only by pedagogical approaches whose design omits any reference to conscience in moral choice. Conscience is equally neglected, and its rights are even violated, by any programme of moral instruction which seeks, either overtly or covertly, to align the students' conscience with a particular body of precepts. Such attempted alignment suggests that conscience itself is more a matter of submissive acquiescence than a matter of circumspection in discerning the universal; more a matter of prompt obedience than of reflection and sincerely informed choice. It should be stressed that choice, here, refers not to matters of taste (as might be the case when one is considering a menu), but to matters of conviction and action.

The answer which is taking shape to our question – Can goodness be taught? – can now be roughly summarised along the following lines: our efforts to teach goodness are likely to come to grief unless they take the form of renewed cooperative learning efforts to discern what goodness is (what human actions might constitute it) in any particular set of circumstances. The fact that as teachers we can involve ourselves with our students in getting such searching efforts underway is precisely the most promising – and the most daunting – prospect, and was briefly mentioned in the above section. It now calls for closer attention. The promising aspect lies in the possibility of building with our students an ethos where critical discernment habitually mingles with generosity of spirit in an adventurous interplay with religious or moral tradition. The daunting aspect lies not merely in the demanding task of bringing about this ethos and interplay, but, more ominously perhaps, in the awareness that the spiritual and moral sensibilities which become nourished in this event – and in a special way those of 'weaker' students – may find themselves in conflict with established moral tradition or established religious authority. History provides us with more than a few famous examples of the point that it is the very success of the moral educator's efforts which invariably irks the representatives of more established pieties.

This open-ended interplay then, this opening anew of the question 'What constitutes goodness?' with each group of students, may appear a radical or iconoclastic answer to our question 'Can goodness be taught?' It seems to imply that there is some goal such as 'moral autonomy' which is independent of established authority and tradition. Perhaps if this thorny point could be resolved, the practical business of *bringing about* the kind of interplay in question might then just be promising and demanding, which it is, rather than daunting, which it should not be. Let us therefore attempt this resolution, albeit in a summary way, in the concluding section.

The Authority of Tradition

The choice of the term 'interplay', above, to describe the kind of approach which is appropriate to moral education, is in no way a casual choice. Firstly, from the side of religious or moral tradition, the word 'interplay' calls attention to the shortcomings of the word 'transmission', which is more commonly used in this context. What is sincerely addressed to the students in an educational interplay calls for their sincere response.

Secondly, from the side of the students, this response is not merely ungenerous, but indeed is mistaken, if it believes itself to be the expression of a radical moral autonomy. The notion of radical moral autonomy is itself an illusion. Every dismissal of the claims of authority and tradition is itself indebted to a contrary tradition; for instance a critical Enlightenment tradition, a revolutionary or nihilist tradition, or even an avant-garde, or sub-cultural tradition. This fact of our inescapable indebtedness to, or dependence on, our forgotten and remembered cultural influences is all too rarely acknowledged. But it is precisely what makes every act of understanding, every interpretation and every judgment a human *interplay*, as distinct from a biological or physical process.

Thirdly, any interplay, as a *play* – of thoughts, arguments, possibilities and so on – takes wing as it were, and gives rise to an absorbing ethos *of its own*. This experience is variously familiar to us from our involvement, even as spectators, in memorable field games, or stage plays; from reading a good book; from participating in a thoughtful discussion; from the attempt to write an article such as this; and not least from the instance of the class which ends with the bell taking both students and teacher by surprise.

The word interplay then is not a semantic decoration, but, in the sense described, shows how we are already actually related to tradition in our everyday dealings, and also provides a clue as to how we might, *educationally*, make such a relation and such dealings more fruitful and enduring. This interplay therefore serves to identify experience which is properly educational, and to distinguish it from that which is not. But how is the question of traditional authority to be tackled in the interplay? This is a rather urgent question for anyone who is a teacher, and such urgency appreciates frank answers. Such an answer, also a thought-provoking one, is suggested in the following words by the German philosopher Hans-Georg Gadamer:

> ... the recognition of authority is always connected with the idea that what authority states is not irrational and arbitrary but can be seen, in principle, to be true. This is the essence of the authority claimed by the teacher, the superior, the expert.[3]

Gadamer's reputation as one of the most distinguished of twentieth-century philosophers rests partly on his cogent restoration of worthiness and dignity to the notions of authority and tradition, thus challenging the more rationalist legacies of a critical Enlightenment spirit. His arguments are especially worthy of our attention here. In particular, the point that needs to be emphasised is the continuing necessity on the part of teachers and students to come, uncoerced, to be of one mind. In the absence of such participatory leadership on the teacher's part, in the absence of the kind of ethos recommended in the preceding pages, authority claims, which can be seen in principle to be true by a community of believers who already share a voluntary avowal of faith, may well be seen to be *in principle unconvincing* by those multitudes of students who do not readily share such an avowal.

It was a growing awareness of the difficulties encountered by moral and religious education in Irish post-primary schools – and of the controversies arising from some of the new attempts to deal with the difficulties – which prompted the present article. By way of summary and conclusion then, the central suggestion of my argument is as follows. Moral and religious traditions, particularly in an era of mass education and radical pluralism, must be encountered in schools on properly educational foundations. The energies that this shift of emphasis releases, the resourcefulness which it encourages and the dramatic engagement which it makes possible, do not mean that the doctrinal contents of a particular tradition must be set aside. Rather they reveal that it is through a singular kind of interplay that these contents now become characteristically encountered in schools: a continually renewed interplay with well-chosen and well-presented examples of life's predicaments and experiences, both hypothetical and real.

Innovations of this kind are a feature of religion teaching in many Irish schools at present. When properly conceived and carried out such teaching in no way interferes with the more explicitly doctrinal and devotional encounter with religious tradition in a church. It recognises however the difference between multitudes and disciples. Some religious authorities may be reluctant to grant that the encounter with religious tradition in schools should be more exploratory than didactic in character. The issue must be seriously faced however and not merely because of the negative point that a failure to do so will yield a dismal harvest. More positively, decisive ecclesiastical and parental support for the approach recommended here might make the task of teachers in tackling the question posed in our title not only promising and demanding, as described in this article. It might also make it fulfilling in an enduring sense for both teachers and students alike.

Notes

1   Martin Buber, 'The Education of Character' in *Between Man and Man,* translated by Ronald Gregor Smith (London: Fontana, 1969), p. 137

2   Ibid., p. 133

3   Hans-Georg Gadamer, *Truth and Method,* translated by Garrett Barden and John Cumming (London: Sheed and Ward, 1975), p. 249.

SIN AND SINFULNESS

— Hugh Connolly —

> We are separated from the mystery, the depth and
> the greatness of our existence. We hear the voice
> of that depth; but our ears are closed. We feel that
> something radical, total and unconditional is
> demanded of us; but we rebel against it, try to
> escape its urgency and will not accept its promise
> ... Sin in its most profound sense, sin as despair
> abounds among us. (Paul Tillich, *The Shaking of
> the Foundations*)

The idea that men and women are morally responsible outside
of particular social practices and conventions of praise and
blame requires at the very least a conception of someone to
whom or something to which they are responsible. To the
Judaeo-Christian mind the immediate tribunal before which the
self is summoned has always been 'conscience upon which is
engraved the law of God'. Norms of responsibility are not
therefore to be to simply considered a matter of individual
choice, or preference, or even social convention. Ultimately the
individual is responsible for herself or himself and the demand
for an authentic coherent ethical stance is thus fundamental to
the moral life.[1]

Ethics in the Christian tradition presupposes therefore
accountability, answerability and responsibility. These notions

are the means by which we also attribute culpability to persons. William Kneale has noted that moral reasoning 'began with an extended use of debt words' and that the language of debt also 'permeates religious discourse'.[2] Religious debate, in turn, and in particular Christian theological ethics, affirms that the coherence and integrity of life is fundamentally linked to what transcends individual and community life – namely God. This insight gives rise to an 'imperative of responsibility' which in some sense articulates the prophetic call to seek justice, love and mercy and walk humbly before God.[3]

Responsibility is therefore a core tenet of the Christian faith – responsibility to oneself, to others and to God. This 'expectation of response', as Niebuhr calls it, encapsulates the Christian imperative to turn away from attitudes and behaviour which demean and destroy the integrity of life and to move toward a moral stance which respects, enhances and promotes right relations. It follows then that failure to respond, failure to strive toward right relations, and failure to be fully responsible is the very essence of sin. This understanding underscores the inadequacy by itself of a 'debt-language' that places too much reliance on those models of law and obedience that tend to characterise and indeed caricature sin in a mechanical, individualistic and actualistic way.

Equally inadequate and unhelpful is the removal of debt language altogether or its replacement with a vocabulary and imagery of fault that relieves persons of all responsibility for their actions. Those psychological, sociological and anthropological approaches that advocate what might be called a 'hard determinism' may succeed in their own terms in lifting the burden of guilt from the shoulders of the sinner. They do this at the cost, though, of severely diluting our understanding of personal freedom and of rendering the ethical dimension well-nigh irrelevant. Wiping out guilt by wiping out the very identity and self-understanding of the person is, by any standards, a rather crude approach. Besides, it would seem that even in terms of the therapeutic goal the strategy is not an entirely successful one.[4] There is a tension, a tensive quality in the concept of sin, which must be respected and retained if the term is not to be devalued and to lose all currency and meaning. The urge to counter a reductionist or deflated account of sin with an expansionist, inflated by ultimately trivialised understanding, is great but must be resisted. The answer must therefore be a more nuanced and synthetic approach.

That said, an important service has been rendered in disentangling, insofar as that is possible, the separate notions of psychological hurt and moral guilt. One can indeed resonate with Denis Potter's observation that all too often religion was 'the wound and not the bandage'.[5] There are 'guilt laden counterfeits of responsibility', human projections which often do 'colonise religious experience' and have the capacity to damage and distort one's image of God and of self. Theological ethics owes a real debt to the modern sciences for their work in exposing such counterfeits and in highlighting the dangers and deficiencies of a theology of sin which becomes too preoccupied with precise deterrents and precise merits. Sin and its remission can too easily be reduced to some manner of theological calculus. Misguided methods of evangelization and exhortation, which either wittingly or unwittingly inflate the understanding of guilt in order to manipulate it, are ultimately perverting the Gospel message of good news and at least to some extent are guilty of producing what Nietzsche called 'a slave morality'.[6]

While it is true that Christianity brings with it a perception of the human being as guilty in its doctrine of Original Sin, this teaching only has relevance in the context of Jesus' liberation of all humanity in his passion and death. Original Sin is therefore essentially about the detection of and 'unmasking of a lie'. The lie in turn, as we have already suggested, is a distorted and flawed self-image which has become internalised and which orients us toward a 'dehumanising self-sufficiency and self-justification'.[7] A wholesome, synthetic account of original sin therefore, far from being at odds with balanced psychological and sociological insights, is in fact engaged in large measures in one and the same project – namely the unmasking of flawed images of God, of self and of the world in which we live. It has been a constant theme of Christian theology from the time of St Paul that divine grace enables us to avoid sin. This implies, however, an acknowledgement of the fact of human wrongdoing, infidelity, selfishness and so forth and of one's accountability for failure. Responsibility and sin are therefore corollaries of each other. In other words, 'to establish the possibility of sin is always simultaneously to confirm the potentialities of human agency and human nature and so, in the final analysis, sin is not an indictment of human nature but a vindication of it.[8] There is a paradox then, an 'inherent irony' in that the very theological concept which more than any other depicts the fragility of the human person and the fragmentary nature of our engagement with the moral life also celebrates the human capacity for change and for the good. This paradox at the heart of the doctrine of sin means that, despite having to grapple with the reality of failure, the teaching bears witness to a very positive underlying theological anthropology.

Viewed in this light it is not altogether surprising that the idea of sin has fallen on such difficult times in the last half-century or so. Modern western thought has tended to abandon the notion of the *Imago Dei* and with it the idea of the intrinsic worth and dignity of the self. Hans Jonas observes: 'the paradox of the modern condition is that this reduction of man's stature, the utter humbling of this metaphysical pride, goes hand in hand with his promotion to quasi-God-like privilege and power'.[9] Whatever about the centrality or otherwise of this 'will to power', there are two very different and competing theological anthropologies or accounts of humanity at play here. The first one, which asserts the sinful nature of the human condition, seems on the face of it to be a gloomy assessment but is in fact the gateway to an exalted understanding of human persons as created in the image of the three-in-one God. Here, each person is viewed as a unique, distinct and unrepeatable person. Each human being has a personal, existential distinctiveness and because of their personal communion with God each partakes in Being, each is therefore more than their biological individuality.

Unlike the second anthropology, which presents the person as an 'individual', a segment or a sub-division of human nature as a whole, the Christian understanding of person is different in that it 'represents not the relationship of a part to the whole but the possibility of summing up the whole in a distinctiveness of relationship in an act of self-transcendence'.[10] In a remarkable way every man and woman encapsulates in his or her own existence the universality of human nature. And this existence is characterised by freedom and distinctiveness. Each human being is given the invitation and the offer of freedom in love and in personal communion. Each may accept or refuse the offer, which is essentially a choice between going along with the process of being or cutting oneself off from being together.

Evidently at the root of these differing anthropologies there are conflicting views of freedom. Modern western liberal thought has gradually moved away from the idea that freedom may be guided by truth about what is good. Some of the existential philosophers (for example John Paul Sartre) have for instance put forward an 'ethic of authenticity' where freedom is understood in a radical way, almost as a law unto itself. Sin, in this philosophical outlook, insofar as it has any meaning, is about failure to break the shackles which hamper authenticity – natural law, religious belief and external value systems. To live authentically one must live radically, and if one lives virtuously one does so, in the words of Camus, only 'by caprice'.

> If there is nothing definitive in nature, no structure in its products, which responds to a purpose, then it is licit to do with it whatever one wants, without by this violating its integrity. For there is no integrity in a nature conceived exclusively in terms of natural science in a nature that is neither created nor creative. [11]

The productive and social changes of the last two centuries have vastly multiplied our choices, and with this has come the championing of the right to choose. Someone has described modernity as the transition from fate to choice. Freedom has been exalted as a core value. But freedom is nevertheless elusive and unsatisfying and is too often confused with independence. The result is the relentless pursuit of a phantom freedom that is in fact only a new form of enslavement.

Homo modernus, whether as a taxpayer, worker or consumer, is increasingly considered a mere digit, a unit of production, consumption or fiscal reckoning. Emptied of the respect, dignity and indeed of the love due to a person, the human being becomes increasingly viewed as a thing. Man turns into a grain of sand and human society becomes a desert. The relentless pursuit of freedom that severs the 'ties' of religion and off-loads the 'prejudices' of tradition and morality leads only to a mirage. Perhaps part of the wrath and bitterness that was unleashed in sometimes anarchic and violent anti-globalisation protests at the beginning of the third millennium was due to this kind of growing disillusionment. There is an increasing realisation that grandiose promises of freedom have led not to real liberation but only to the dull conformity of fashion and to the influences of the utterly hollow and ephemeral. In the same way the irony of the Judaeo-Christian stance is that it is an ethic that at first glance appears constricting and even suffocating but which in fact holds out the promise of real freedom.

The key of course is in the acceptance of the human being as essentially relational. Viewed in this light, the ties that really bind us are not bonds of imprisonment at all but bonds of attachment of communion and of love. The freedom we enjoy is a 'created freedom', and therefore the fundamental choice is not really between dependence and independence: it is a decision between a living dependence, which is open to growth and development, and a dead dependence, which refuses to acknowledge our creature status and therefore cuts us off from the sources of life.

These competing versions of freedom were also to form the backdrop to the 1994 papal encyclical *Veritatis Splendor* and to the episode of the rich young man's encounter with Jesus (Mt 19:16-22) which inspired and informed the encyclical's reflections on this topic. Jesus' response to the young man's enquiry about what he must do to gain eternal life was prefaced by a reminder that human good or moral good finds its ultimate source in the absolute good – the 'one who is good'. The aspirations to freedom and to the good are but particular articulations of the desire for the infinite. In this way 'human freedom bursts open to dimensions for which only God is the answer because only the absolute Good satisfies the restless heart'.[12]

Evidently future receptivity to a doctrine or even a sense of sin are inextricably linked to humanity's willingness to remain open to the transcendent. Sin can only be truly understood in terms of the living and personal bond between humanity and God, which is in turn the foundation of all human relationships. That is why 'the second commandment is like the first'. To love one's neighbour as oneself is, above all, to respect the freedom that he or she holds from God. As Paul explained in his image of the 'Body of Christ', each member of the living organism develops freely so long as it is intimately joined to the rest of the body. So the foundation for the injunction to love one's neighbour as oneself is the intimate relationship and relatedness of human beings. I love you not because you are giving me this or that, but because in a certain sense I am you and you are I in communion with our common source which is the triune God. This is the idea that is the common focus, the synthesis and the regulating centre of all our individual freedoms.[13]

If such are the philosophical and theological underpinnings of the Judaeo-Christian account of sin it should also be acknowledged that it has been the genius of the same tradition to propose side by side with the formal doctrine of repentance a tradition of sacrament, ritual and religious practice. This has provided another means by which to understand and to concretely experience the mystery of sin and conversion. Recourse is made here above all to the language of symbol, metaphor and bodily enactment (which is the language of Scripture after all) in its attempt to embrace in a holistic and accessible way the human experience of wrongdoing, repentance and reorientation. In more recent times this kind of indirect language has attracted the attention of philosophers such as Paul Ricoeur and Réné Girard who have shown how symbolic and mimetic communication can speak beyond logic to the human heart. In particular they have drawn attention to what Ricoeur calls the 'double intentionality' of metaphor, that is, the literal and latent layers of meaning.

Symbols and metaphors give rise to a 'spontaneous hermeneutics', a struggle toward newer and fuller levels of meaning. This insight has led to several attempts in recent years to revitalise and re-energise the theological language of sin by re-examining the underpinning imagery. More particularly, these theological initiatives have sought to shift the emphasis away from juridical/criminal models which tend to reinforce a highly individualistic anthropology toward more therapeutic and communitarian paradigms which successfully evoke the universal struggle with the crippling and disintegrating power of sin.[14] These approaches are at once more coherent with the wider scope of biblical wisdom and more receptive also to the interdisciplinary, synthetic approaches that are found in recent theological debate and research. But they are only useful insofar as they are tolerant of the actual blend of metaphor and imagery, which emerges from the scriptural and doctrinal tradition. There is no one paradigm or metaphor that holds the definitive key to the understanding of sin. Each must dialogue, modify and, as Ricoeur puts it, 'struggle' with the others. Any attempt to underplay the 'juridical' model for instance would be just as misconceived and misguided as the well-documented tendency to overlay what it formerly was.

Among these theological voices the contribution of those writing from the political, ecological, liberationist and feminist perspectives have also been very much to the fore. While feminist theologians have tended to concentrate less on the theme of sin and more on the patriarchal identification of women with sin, their work has on occasions lucidly demonstrated how prone our religious imagery and theological paradigms are to distortion and bias. Such bias they contend may also express itself in ethical theory and in the basic understanding of the moral life. Spiritual and moral machismo, for instance, may be found in inordinate preoccupation with victory over individual sins to the neglect of responsibility for nourishing and nurturing relationships.[15] Some critiques go much further and argue that there is a tendency within traditional conceptions of morality to legitimate so-called 'feminine virtues' thereby actually perpetuating injustice and oppression. Whatever the validity of these claims, there is no doubt that feminist thinkers have done a great service in highlighting the 'sin' of sexism. The blatant dishonesty at the root of a 'belief that gender is the primary determinant of human characteristics, traits, abilities and talents and that sexual differences produce an inherent superiority of a particular sex'[16] has been exposed for once and for all.

This theological critique also raises questions about the accuracy of *hubris* as a type for universal sin since this very concept 'mirrors chiefly the experience of men' who aspire to positions of power and influence.[17] But perhaps this criticism implies a too facile identification between *hubris* and the traditional Judaeo-Christian conception of sin. The latter, as we have tried to point out, was more concerned with an integral account of human sinfulness, of which *hubris* was but one expression. To be sure, the classical theological conceptualisation of sin has its limitations. Nevertheless the underlying understanding of sin as a negation of who one truly is called to be rendered this theology at least potentially open and receptive to new experiences of sin such as those evoked today by those who reflect feminist, ecological and social concerns. What is more, there would seem to be some validity in the arguments of those who suggest that the notion that 'men sin through pride and women through weakness' is itself a stereotype which has become a little dated at the beginning of the third millennium.[18]

Even so, patriarchal structures and sexist attitudes are still a reality in society generally and in Christian churches and communities more particularly. Like liberation theologians, feminists have drawn inspiration from the central prophetic tradition of Judaeo-Christian ethics which emphasised God's defence of the oppressed, as well as the need to criticise oppressive power structures in society and the importance of recognising ideological elements in religious belief. They have also critiqued an overly spiritualised account of original sin that fails to respect the 'earthedness' and bodiliness of human life. Reuther argues:

> The Big Lie tells us that we are strangers and sojourners on this planet, that our flesh, our blood, our instincts for survival are our enemies. We have fallen to this earth and into this clay through accident or sin. We must spend our lives suppressing our hungers and thirsts and shunning our fellow beings so that we can dematerialise and fly away to the stars.[19]

It is one thing to acknowledge with the author of the Letter to the Hebrews that 'we have here no abiding city'; it is quite another to use this as an excuse for avoiding the individual and societal responsibilities which are an essential part of our human calling.

But feminists such as Reuther do see within the tradition seeds of a new way of imaging God, sin, conversion and so forth. They point to the maternal love and compassion of Yahweh, the presence of Wisdom conceived of as a feminine reality, and the as-yet underdeveloped female imagery associated with the work of the Holy Spirit. Although there is a great variety and divergence of opinion and of intensity among feminist reflections on sin, one senses here a thrust toward a more fully human and inclusive understanding of fault and finitude. Construed in this way the universal sinful tendency 'consists essentially in denying the co-humanity of the others one experiences'.[20] Such reflections have made an invaluable contribution to unmasking the dehumanising side of sin. In doing so they are broadly at one with theologians who argue that sin is essentially about refusing the invitation to play our part in the human family's journey towards becoming more fully human.[21] The fact that Christian theology, and in particular its reflection on sin and evil, has until very recently been constructed predominantly by men, to the near exclusion of the experience and insights of women, inevitably means that there is essential corrective work to be done. Only thus can theology itself hope to be freed from the dehumanising effects of sin.

At the same time, a new awareness of the fragility and delicate ecological balance of the environment has led to increased reflection on the human duty of stewardship for all creation and what this means in terms of concrete individual and collective moral responsibility. Here there are really parallels with the classical Christian view of justice as right relationships. Sally McFague explains: 'If the most basic meaning of justice is fairness then from an ecological point of view justice means sharing the limited resource of our common space.'[22] Ecological sin is quite simply then refusing or neglecting to share these resource with those who are most in need of them. It is also a failure to recognise the inherent goodness of the natural world. That goodness is a deeply rooted conviction throughout Scripture. After each of Yahweh's acts of creation the creation accounts recall that 'he found it very good' (Gen 1:31). Similarly the Psalms proclaim that 'the earth is the Lord's and all that is in it; the world and those who live in it, for he has founded it on the seas, and established it on the rivers (Ps 24:1-2).

There is a pervasive recognition here that the world is not ours and that human beings are part of the created world. Made in the image of likeness of God, human beings are to reflect God to the rest of creation, to look after and care for the world and its natural resources. There is the implication here of a caretaking role, a duty of stewardship, which is part of a grace-filled respect for the integrity of all creation. Such an attitude is directly opposed to the purely utilitarian stance, which considers natural resources to be expendable and disposable commodities. It is also a relational attitude, an attitude that calls for a rediscovery of our connectedness to and dependence on the earth. This sense of justice toward all creation had once found expression in the ancient Jewish tradition of the Sabbath law and the Jubilee Year. There was a sense of allowing the earth to replenish its resources and restore its energies during a fallow period. For theologians like McFague, Dorr, McDonagh and others, traditions like these bespeak a practical and ethical wisdom, which understands that the relationship between the earth and human beings, like the relationship between persons, must be one of mutual giving and receiving.

Failure to respect this mutuality and reciprocity is a failure to act honestly and is therefore sinful. 'A land ethic that aims to preserve the integrity, stability and beauty of the biotic community is an example of living appropriately on the land and refusing to live the lie that we are the conquerors, the possessors and the masters of the earth.'[23] One can speak meaningfully therefore of ecological sin and of the need to encourage awareness of sustainability issues. *Sollicitudo Rei Socialis* argues for a greater realisation of 'the limits of available resources and of the need to respect the integrity and cycles of nature', as well as the 'mutual connection in an ordered system, which is precisely the cosmos'.

Reverence for the earth is an ethical and religious imperative that touches our self-understanding in a profound way and which asks searching moral questions of our individual and collective lifestyles. Insofar as we refuse to recognise these questions or reject their import or fail to answer them in an adequate way, we also disregard the perennial summons to 'act justly, love tenderly and walk humbly with our God'. This rejection is what we have learned to call sin.

The fields of political theology and liberation theology are the locus of some other recent attempts to contextualise the concept of sin. As with the ecological and the feminist perspectives, one cannot do justice to the breadth of industry and scholarship being undertaken in this field in a brief *tour d'horizon* such as this. In large measures the preoccupations of these theologies such as those of Johann Baptist Metz and Dorothee Sölle have sought to develop theological reflection on sin and guilt in the context of contemporary social relationships in the modern world. Their approach sets out specifically to challenge and critique the individual bias, which is a part of modern western culture. Metz's theology was influenced by his traumatic experiences of the Second World War. He and Sölle raised the question of the suffering of innocent victims and of the large groups of people who are denied the opportunity of becoming 'subjects' due to political and social repression. According to them, there is a need for people to liberate themselves from the structures that impede their integral growth and development. What is required is a collective conversion, an 'anthropological revolution' where people emancipate themselves from the influences of 'privatism' and from the sinful tendencies of consumption and domination. This can only be achieved when collectively we are prepared to leave behind the competitiveness and egotism of our 'success ethic' and to realise the full implications of our status as essentially social beings. According to this view we must commit to an acceptance of responsibility for ourselves, for the human family and for the world.

> When Christianity takes its place in the movement
> towards the development of world-wide

community it will be able to express, in and for that great community, its understanding of a solidarity that is free from violence and hatred.[24]

It is not hard to see how so-called political theology became the forerunner of so many contextualised theologies in the latter half of the twentieth century that were to lay great emphasis on the 'primacy of praxis' and the search for universal justice. That said, despite the radical tone of this approach there is also recognition here of what Metz calls the 'eschatological proviso'. This is an acknowledgement that God's promise of salvation will never be fully realised within history and that only the 'God of the living and the dead' ultimately can fulfil the promise of history.

Western political theologies were to provide much inspiration for liberation theology, especially in their critique of a 'privatised ethic' that only camouflaged the true causes of sin. Many of the liberation theologians went for a distinction between social sin and individual sin which had social repercussions. They tended to do this by pointing to the differences between sin understood as 'communal', that is pertaining to the interpersonal dimension of primary relationships, and as 'societal' sin, which concerns the more complex, impersonal and structural secondary relationship. The human being was therefore at the nexus of a set of two-way mutually impacting relationships, each of which was vulnerable to the damaging and destructive effects of sin.

Advances in human, political and economic science also provided the opportunity for a penetrating analysis of each of these relationships, thus bringing them into the theological foreground. In this way society's mechanisms were laid bare with the birth of the social sciences. They teach us that poverty, hunger, ignorance and misery don't just happen but are the demonstrable results of socio-economic and political relationships.[25] And so liberation theologies argued for a social prismatic in all theological accounts of sin that would serve as a necessary antidote and corrective to a too-privatised moral climate and culture. They placed the poor at the centre, as those who most embodied the hope for change and liberation. They also reworked the great biblical motifs exemplified by the Exodus event as well as the New Testament emphasis on Jesus' compassion toward the poor. This they saw as only underscoring the importance of liberation in Christian life. In other words, liberations had to be seen in concrete, practical and tangible, as well as spiritual, ways.

The sheer multiplicity of views within the liberation perspective makes any general comment on their theology of sin quite difficult. At one level it is but a reflection of the broad post-conciliar trends towards a renewed appreciation of the dignity of the human person and of the demands of social justice and is therefore advocating a more thorough and integral understanding of sin in all its dimensions. At another level some of its more radical exponents have been accused of substituting political salvation in history for external salvation and of underplaying 'the full ambit of sin whose first effect is to introduce disorder into the relationship between God and man and cannot be restricted to "social sin"'.[26] In any event, liberation theology has unquestionably been instrumental in the repositioning of theological emphases from the universal to the particular, the privileged to the deprived and the systematic to the narrative and performative.[27] It has drawn much-needed attention to the disastrous human suffering caused by unjust institutions and structures, and has urged humanity, and especially faith communities, to take a responsible rule in fighting injustice and building solidarity. Perhaps though it is here that the advocates of social sin, understood in the 'hard' sense, are on their weakest ground. If one is really to urge responsibility in social justice one must be prepared first to acknowledge the facts of responsibility and accountability as human possibilities and realities, otherwise the same determinisms which explain why sin will just as surely erode the very grounds for social action and responsibility.

If there is a common strand or unifying theme in the so-called contextualised theologies it is their insistence on sin as opposition to Jesus' message, where kingdom is no mere extension of intrinsic human possibilities but a radical restructuring of inter-human relationships grounded in justice. What is more, this justice is not simply about corrective action or redress for wrongs that have been done; instead it is truly restorative and re-creative. Sin is understood as nothing less than the rejection of God's plan for filial and fraternal relationships, while justice on the other hand 'concretises the praxis of love and so realises the Kingdom'.[28]

In this optic there is room for much common ground between classical and contemporary theology because each in its own way presents sin as the human failure, whether individual or collective, to be what one is called to be and to realise the fullness of one's individual potentialities. A more dynamic understanding of creation and of the human person can thus allow the classical and the contemporary views to speak meaningfully to each other.

It is here perhaps that the personalist and process perspectives are at their most valuable. While Boethius' definition of the human being as 'an individual substance of a rational nature' has proved a timeless insight and has become the bedrock of much ethical reflection and rights language and legislation, it does not capture in itself the fullness of the Judaeo-Christian concept of the person. In particular it fails to do justice to the 'dynamic nature of human existence, with its movement toward the fulfiling of aims or goals'.[29]

One thinks here of Amos' concept of justice as represented

by the river gently growing deeper and flowing toward the sea, of the case of an incremental line of advance and progression throughout the moral life. Perhaps there is a sense too in which the moral life may be seen as a task of becoming human, a task in which one is called to co-create with God. One is invited also to accept responsibility for one's life, and to gradually realise agapeic love both in one's own person and in communion with others. Understood in this light, sin is, above all, the failure to incarnate love and to cooperate with God in a great act of giving birth to a new *koinonia*. The recreative, regenerative process takes place first and foremost in the human heart, and all that is required is the cooperation of human free will – the willingness to surrender one's aspirations to self-sufficiency and to accept God's love and the implications of that love in outreach to others.

This dynamic and synthetic view of creation and of human person sees the *Imago Dei* as at once gift and task. Each human being has been created in the image and likeness of the triune God and is therefore conferred with an undeniable dignity, but each is also called to make real that 'communion of love' which is the hallmark of the same triune God in his or her own life. This is the awesome but also potentially tragic adventure of human nature. Sin therefore represents one possible expression of that freedom which is ultimately 'a refusal, whether small or great, of human destiny in its noblest reach'.[30]

Columbanus, the great Irish pilgrim monk, and author of a penitential handbook, once suggested in one of his sermons that each human being may ultimately determine the 'picture' that is to be painted in and through their lives. 'Let us not be the painters of another's image ... for righteousness and righteousness ... are opposed to one another. Then lest perhaps we should import into ourselves despotic images let Christ paint his image in us.'[31] According to this view the moral life works gradually either to confirm the imprint of the *Imago Dei* upon one's entire being or else to slowly replace it with the image of the tyrant – to whom or to which one has become enslaved.

Even in these earliest theological reflections there was evidence of a synthetic, integral and holistic approach. There was also keen awareness of the continuous as well as the immediate aspects of moral behaviour. Indeed, it has also been the tenor of the vast learning and practical wisdom of the Christian tradition to regard both the immediate and continuous dimensions as co-essential aspects of the moral life. In other words, one has to allow each of these dimensions to co-exist in creative and complementary tension.

Recent theology has therefore sought to root its reflections on sin in a more adequate synthetic and integral understanding of the human person. It has rediscovered the dramatic and incredible assertion at the heart of Matthew's account of the final judgment that 'as often as you did this to one of the least of these my brothers and sisters you did it also to me!' (Mt 25:31-46). To love others is therefore to love God, and conversely to fail others is to fail God. Sin is therefore not only a moral fault but also a religious failure. Recovery from sin challenges us in turn to a renewal of faith, to a renewed acceptance of the fact that the path away from sin and toward healing and wholeness cannot be travelled alone. Growth out of sin is but another way of describing our own personal part in the ongoing story of humankind as it continues its struggle toward the realisation of the kingdom of God.[32] It is here too that the lament for sin and the sadness of the contrite heart become a joyful sorrow. For in truth we are only able to mourn and lament when we really appreciate what we have lost. A genuine grasp of the 'reality of sin' becomes therefore the first moment of our encounter with God. This is the moment when we truly discover the awesome extent of His love.

Notes

1 W. Schweiker, *Responsibility and Christian Ethics* (Cambridge: University Press, 1995), 73f.

2 W. Kneale, 'The Responsibility of Criminals', in James Rachels (ed.) *Moral Problems: A Collection of Philosophical Essays* (New York: Harper & Row, 1971), 172, cited in Schweiker, op. cit. p. 75.

3 Schweiker, op. cit. p. 133.

4 Karl Menninger's *Whatever became of Sin?* remains a remarkable insight and stimulating essay on the importance of sin beyond the strictly religious and theological worlds. See Menninger, K., *Whatever Became of Sin?* (New York: Hawthorn, 1973).

5 See D. Potter, *Seeing the Blossom* (Faber 1994), 5, cited in Phillips, D., 'Exposing the Wound: A Christian Reflection on Guilt' *Downside Review*, 1999, 408.

6 F. Nietzche, *On the Genealogy of Morals* (Trans. W. Kaufmann), (New York: Vintage, 1989).

7 See K.T. Kelly, *New Directions in Moral Theology* (London/NY: Chapman, 1992), 120f.

8 J. McKenna, 'The Possibility of Social Sin', *Irish Theological Quarterly* (60), 1994.

9 H. Jonas, 'Contemporary Problems in Ethics from a Jewish Perspective' in *Philosophical Essays* (Prentice Hall, 1972), 172, cited in Schweiker, op. cit. p. 73.

10 C. Yannaras, *The Freedom of Morality* (New York: St Vladimir's Press, 1996), 21f.

11 H. Jonas, 'Dalla fede antica all uomo tecnologico', *Il Molino* (Bologna, 1991) 263, cited in May, W.E. 'Veritatas Splendor: An Overview' Communio, 1994, 21.

12 W.E. May, op. cit. p. 23.

13 G. Thibon et al., *Christianisme et Liberté*, (Paris: Arthéme Fayard, 1952), 7ff.

14 See, for instance, P.T McCormick, *Sin as Addiction* (New York: Paulist Press, 1989); my own *The Irish Penitentials* (Dublin: Four Courts Press, 1995); K. O'Kelly, *The Changing Paradigms of Sin* (New Blackfriars, November 1989) and K. Cronin, 'Illness, Sin and Metaphor', *Irish Theological Quarterly,* 61 (1995).

15 See C. Gilligan, *In a Different Voice* (Harvard: University Press, 1983), 19f.

16 R.E. Coll, *Christianity and Feminism in Conversation* (Connecticut Twenty Third Publications, 1994), p. 112.

17 L. Scherzberg, *Sünde und Gnade in der Feministischen Theologie* (Mainz, 1990); see also Van Heijst, A., 'Sin as the Disruption of Relationship' in F. Vosman and K.W. Merks (eds) *Aiming at Happiness* (Kampen, 1996), p. 141.

18 See Denise L. Carmody, *Christian Feminist Theology* (Oxford: Blackwell, 1995), p. 113.

19 R. Reuther, *Sexism and God-Talk* (Boston: Beacon Press, 1983).

20 L.S. Cahill, *Sex, Gender and Christian Ethics* (Cambridge University Press, 1996), p. 118.

21 See, for example, C.T. Daly, *Creation and Redemption* (Dublin: Gill & Macmillan, 1988).

22 S. McFague, *The Body of God* (London: SCM, 1993), p. 116. NB: I have relied here extensively on McFague's excellent presentation and analysis of ecological sin.

23 McFague, op. cit.; see also Leopold, A., *A Sand County Almanac* (Oxford University Press, 1949), pp. 224–5.

24 J.B. Metz, *Faith in History and Society* (New York: Seabury, 1980).

25 A. Moser, 'Sin as Negation of the Kingdom', *Theology Digest* 30:1, Spring (1982), p. 29.

26 Congregation for the Doctrine of the Faith, *Libertatis Nuntius* (London: Catholic Truth Society, 1984), p. 14.

27 See E. McDonagh, 'An Irish Theology and the Influence of Particulars' in *Irish Challenges to Theology* (Dublin: Dominican Publications, 1986), pp. 102–29.

28 Moser, op. cit. p. 28.

29 N. Pittenger, *Cosmic Love and Human Wrong* (New York: Paulist Press, 1978), p. 13: an excellent essay on the implications of process thinking for the doctrine of sin.

30 Pittenger, op. cit. p. 44.

31 *Sermon*, XI.

32 See K.T. Kelly, 'Saints or Sinners? Towards a Spirituality of Growth Out of Sin', in *From a Parish Base* (London DLT, 1999), p. 166.

A FEMINIST APPROACH TO SIN

— Elizabeth Rees —

For some years I have been grappling with our traditional concept of sin. I have tried without success to see myself as a prodigal daughter or a found sheep. I do not feel like a saved sinner. Normally I postpone dealing with this issue, hoping that along with developing maturity an awareness of sin might grow. The saints were fond of calling themselves great sinners, so perhaps a conviction of sinfulness just grows. But what if the saints were simply grasping for words to describe the immense differentness between God and themselves? What if they were simply searching for a way to describe how immensely alive and loving God is?

Many Christians believe they are saved sinners, and I have met a few people who have indeed experienced a radical conversion from one lifestyle to another. However, I believe that others, like me, were brought up as controlled, well-behaved little people who would need an abnormal dose of courage to go out and do anything outstandingly harmful to anyone. Certainly, I am not at every moment fully stretched to the point of my fullest capacity to love, but I do not believe that a human person is built to do so or required to do so. Yet I believe I am normally open to caring for myself and others, simply because I am alive and relatively emotionally stable.

I look around the members of my own family – those people whom I have know longest and most intimately. Who is sinful? I consider my disabled sister: each day she struggles against unbearable levels of pain and emerges smiling, caring and faithful. Each day she finds new ways to be creative and to love. Does God see her as sinful? I doubt it. At the other end of the spectrum, I consider my mother: fearful, dominating, manipulative. Each day she finds a hundred ways to insult her husband; each night she struggles vainly to put her worried mind to sleep. Does God see her as sinful? Probably not, for he knows how emotionally limited her choices are, how hard she struggles for affirmation in the face of inner despair, and how unpredictably violent her own childhood was. Surely God smiles at her in blessing as she fills my bag with flowers, jam and cakes and waves me goodbye for another month.

If I do not see myself as sinful, how do I view myself? More like a growing plant. A plant is not good or bad; it simply grows according to its nature and in response to its environment. In healthy soil, with rain and sunshine, it will grow well and strong. In adverse conditions, it will still try to grow. I do not feel either virtuous or bad, but I know I am alive and I care deeply about growing. I respect, nurture and cherish my growing shoot, and I hope to grow into the fullness which God has in mind for me. And to the extent that I am alive, my life will flow into others too.

If we are, by and large, doing our best to grow, given our emotional limitations, are we then sinful – literally, full of sin? I recognise the existence of serious sin in the actions of some persons, such that early Christians instituted Confession as a second baptism for serious offenders. At the other end of the scale, I cannot see that the harassed mother who goes to Confession on Saturday morning and accuses herself of being irritable is doing much good, for irritability is the normal human response of a person who is overstretched. With some hesitance I have moved away from Confession, though firmly committed to spiritual direction and counselling.

If sin is thus demythologised, what about forgiveness? Too often I hear forgiveness explained as a psychological short-cut. The process becomes one of: 'Ask God to suppress your anger at so-and-so's behaviour. Then you can be nice to them.' This is unhealthy. I need to both experience and allow anger at what another person does to me. According to my maturity I may be able to choose whether or not to blast off the other, depending on whether this action might or might not be beneficial. I do not like to claim the word 'forgive'. More accurate would be 'understand and accept'. If I make the effort to understand what causes the other's behaviour, I will to some extent accept it. God forgives; I wonder whether human beings can appropriate the word.

If I am not full of sin, then what of the redemption? Is Jesus on the cross redeeming me, buying me back? Why is he on the cross at all? Historically, because Jesus, a good man, provoked some self-righteous men to a murderous fury. Cosmologically, because Jesus entered with every fibre of his being into the work of transforming chaos into form, decay into new life. And each person is involved in the same struggle, both as victim and creator.

What happens then to sin? Here is Thomas Merton's view, which escaped his monastic censors:

> The voice of God is heard in paradise:
> What was vile has become precious. What is now precious was never vile. I have always known the vile as precious: for what is vile I know not at all.

What was cruel has become merciful. What is
now merciful was never cruel. I have always
overshadowed Jonas with my mercy and cruelty I
know not at all. Have you had sight of me, Jonas
my child? Mercy within mercy within mercy. I
have forgiven the universe without end, because I
have never known sin.

(The Sign of Jonas)

Is all this merely poetic licence, or is there an alternative to a
theology dominated by death and sin? In the last twenty years
there has been considerable research into early Christian
theology, as Syriac scholars have become familiar with a corpus
of previously unexplored Christian texts. Early disciples of
Luke took literally his Master's injunction to set you two by
two, and with nowhere to lay their heads they set out through
Syria to proclaim the Good News. While St Paul brought his
educated mind to bear on the mysteries of God, and preached
them in the cities of Greece, Rome and Asia Minor, early
followers of the apostles went through Syria, preaching the
Good News with an emphasis on life rather than death. What
follows is derived from the work of Gabriele Winkler, probably
the greatest Syriac scholar of today.

In Syria, the common word for 'Saviour' is 'Life-giver'. The
Syriac text of the Gospels is worded this way. There is a Syriac
equivalent of the Greek 'sōtēr' (saviour), but the word 'Life-
giver' normally appears instead. The word 'Saviour' conveys a
negative concept of being freed, rescued or saved from
something, while the word 'Life-giver' conveys a positive
concept of causing and bestowing life. In the Syriac New
Testament, the Greek verbs meaning 'to deliver', 'to redeem'
and 'to save' are rendered differently using words which mean
'to give life', 'to make alive' and 'to cause to live'.

In the nativity story, the angels say to the shepherds: 'To you this day is born the Saviour' in the Greek text (Lk 2:11), but the Syriac and Georgian text renders the passage: 'To you is born this day the One who makes alive.' The Greek text translates John the Baptist's exhortation in Luke 3:6 as: 'All flesh will see the salvation of God', where the Syriac says: 'All flesh will see the life of God.' When Jesus cures the woman with a haemorrhage (in Mt 9:22) the Greek text has him say: 'Your faith has saved you.' The Syriac, Armenian and Georgian texts have him say: 'Your faith has made you alive.' When Christ instructs his followers in Matthew 10:22, the Greek text has him say: 'He who endures to the end will be saved', but the Syrian, Armenian and Georgian texts say: 'He who endures will be living.'

In the Syrian tradition, the positive notion of 'bestowing life' prevails over the negative Greek notion of 'being saved' from something. The Syrian ascetics followed the wonderful 'bestower of life', the 'one who causes to live', through a radical turning away from what Jesus pronounced dead, when he said: 'Leave the dead to bury their own dead' (Lk 9:60). The Syrian ascetics speak of the great power of love: they willingly accept uprooting from everything in order to become newly rooted in the life-begetting Spirit of Jesus the Life-giver. Their understanding of baptism was correspondingly different from that of the Greeks: it was seen as a spiritual birth, corresponding to original creation of the world. Thus the earliest form of Christian baptism was oriented towards new life in the Spirit (based on the outpouring of the Spirit upon Jesus when he emerged from the Jordan) and the story of creation (when the Spirit hovered over the formless watery void and poured life upon it). St John's Gospel proclaims this theology of being born of water and the Spirit (Jn 3).

This theology has nothing in common with the 'death mysticism' of St Paul's letter to the Romans: 'We are dead to sin, so how can we continue to live in it? ... When we were baptised in Christ Jesus we were baptised in his death ... Our former selves have been crucified with him to destroy this sinful body and to free us from the slavery of sin ...' (Rom 6:1 ff). This Pauline theology had no importance for the Syrians of the first four centuries. Their emphasis was the reintegration of creation into its original unity. This transfiguration in the One who is Christ the 'Life-giver', the 'Bestower of life', the 'One who causes to live' is brought about by the Spirit of holiness, who rested originally on Jesus in the Jordan, and now rests on all who are born anew from the waters of baptism. St Ephrem describes this in his sixth epiphany hymn:

> The Spirit rose from on high
> and hallowed the waters by his hovering [over them] at the baptism of John.
> He left everything and rested upon the One.
> Now, however, he descended and rested upon all
> who are born from the waters.

Ephrem understands that Jesus reopened paradise by his baptism, and speaks of Adam not in terms of original sin but in terms of original blessing. At baptism we clothe ourselves, according to Ephrem, with the splendour of Adam:

> My spirit carried me to the Jordan [i.e. to Jesus' baptism] and I saw the miracle as it unfolded:
> the splendid Bridegroom
> who will take and consecrate the bride
> at the wedding feast ...
> a bridal chamber which is not fleeting
> you have received, my brothers.
> And into the splendour of Adam
> did you clothe yourself today.

> (Hymns 5, 6)

If we follow the Syrian Ephrem's thinking to its conclusion, and posit a world of original blessing rather than a world of original sin, then we do not have to be so concerned with wiping sin out. And we need to remember that the concept of original sin was posited in order to produce a reason for the baptising of infants, which became widespread only after Constantine made Christianity the state religion (if baptising meant bringing out of sin, there must be a kind of sin out of which babies could be brought). And while it is a broad and long-standing pietist tradition that God likes us to approach Him as sinners constantly in need of mercy, it is quite possible that God loves us anyhow, and likes us to enjoy the goodness which He gives us.

'Mercy within mercy within mercy' is a description of God's deep motherly tenderness. In Merton's view of sin we do not encounter the God of patriarchy, the 'just judge' who 'weighs our sins in the balance'. Julian of Norwich describes sin from a similar viewpoint when she writes: 'In God's sight we do not fall; in our sight we do not stand' (*Revelations of Divine Love,* ch. 82). God our mother looks on us, she says, 'with pity, not with blame'.

God may not see us as sinful, but we are human and we do fail one another. In discussions with mothers whose children are preparing for First Confession and First Communion, I generally pick up considerable unease about sin. These mothers have been put in a double bind by a Church which first taught them, 'Sin is something which at all costs you must not do', and later taught them 'Sin is something we all do.' If we must never do what we all do, we are trapped. Today's middle-aged Catholics were taught as children: 'Sin is wrong; you must not sin.' They were taught a theology of perfection: our task is to become perfect. Later, these people were taught according to a different, reality-based theology: we are all flawed or incomplete; sin is part of us all.

The Church did not, however, teach us that we are often sinned against; we are often victims of others' sin. In a patriarchal Church and society, women are sinned against. We women cannot have a realistic view of our own sin until we can acknowledge the extent to which we are victims of the sins of others. In her exhilarating book, *Women Who Run with the Wolves*, Clarissa Pinkola Estes describes how she once made a 'scapecoat', using materials and symbols to represent the insults and abuse which she had received from others. When she finally put on her scapecoat she found, to her surprise, that she felt good wearing it, proud that although she had received so much abuse from others, she could sit lightly with it and still tackle life smiling. She had named others' sins against her.

I decided to make a scapecoat when I was working on a retreat team. I used a discarded sheet, cutting it up into a circular cape with a hole for my head. I laid it out in our 'creative arts' room to decorate it, and decided to write on it the various insults I felt I carried. To my surprise, women retreatants whom I didn't know and who normally prayerfully ignored one another came up, pointing to different pieces of my scapecoat saying, 'Yes! This is me too!' For the first time, I gained some insight into the ancient Jewish concept of the scapegoat, whom they drove into the desert, bearing the sins of the nation. I understood too the words of John the Baptist: 'Look! There is the Lamb of God who takes away the sins of the world.' It is important for women to acknowledge their role as bearers of sin in today's Church and world.

There is always the danger, however, of becoming a scapegoat in the debased sense of the term, by becoming a victim. It is so difficult for women to stay in touch with their power, and refuse to be trampled on. In an acted-out penitential liturgy, a group divided into two parts: the victims who lay on the floor, and the oppressors who stood over them, ready to strike. The victims asked to be struck yet again. Then the whole group prayed for mercy both for the times when we oppress others and for the times when we allow ourselves to be oppressed.

Women know what it feels like to 'bear the sins of the world': the tired mother who answers her crying baby night after night, the single parent who goes without necessities so that her children can eat enough, the wife raped by her husband, the woman who sells her body to pay school fees. These women share in the action of Jesus, the Lamb of God, who bears the sin of the world. Women who struggle to bring life to a Church which tells them: 'Go away!' – these women are helping God to redeem the world; they are giving birth to a new creation of love and freedom. These women know sin, because they are engaged in redeeming the world.

I believe that women cannot acknowledge themselves as sinners until they recognise that they are sinned against. Furthermore, women need to gratefully realise that, in union with Jesus, they are helping to bear the world's sin; they are taking away the sins of the world. Women are ready to confess their sins only perhaps when they are open to the mystery and grandeur of the Forgiveness which they already live out.

HIV AND CATHOLIC THEOLOGY

— Julie Clague —

The Bible is the chief inspirational resource that Christians draw upon. The starting point for understanding humane living (Christian morality) is the dialogical relationship between humankind and God – especially as God has been revealed in the person of Jesus Christ. God has revealed love for us – something that is captured in the Old Testament stories of God's covenant with the people of Israel who were brought out of bondage in Egypt.

God's love continues to be revealed in the incarnation, through Jesus' words and actions. The natural thing for humans to do who understand the world and its creatures as something created and loved by God, enveloped in this relationship, is to respond to this loving initiative in kind: we profess our faith in the way we live our lives.

In the Old Testament, two books of the Pentateuch carry a summary of what this means in practice: 'Hear O Israel: The Lord our God is one Lord; and you shall love the Lord your God with all your heart, and with all your soul, and with all your might' (Deut 6:4-5) and ' ... you shall love your neighbour as yourself: I am the Lord' (Lev 19:18).

In the New Testament as a response to a Pharisee's request for the greatest commandment in the Law Jesus identifies the Deuteronomy command. The second is the Leviticus command to love neighbour as self. These two commands are singled out by Jesus as the greatest commands through which all other laws must be understood and interpreted: 'On these two commandments depend all the law and the prophets' (Mt 22:38-40).

In other words, Jesus pointed to the two chief ways that we can make this response: through love of God and love of neighbour. This is what life in Christ involves. It must honour God and serve persons. The earliest Christians found this a crucial teaching of Jesus and it is repeated throughout the Gospels and in Paul. In other words, we are misunderstanding the practical implications of the Gospel if we interpret it to demand behaviour that is dehumanising and violates the good of human persons.

In terms of moral wisdom, one of the classic texts is that of the Decalogue. The Ten Commandments can be considered paradigmatic summaries of the humane response to God's initiative, for they are set in the liberative context of God delivering the Hebrews from slavery in Egypt. The biblical texts that contain the Decalogue capture the dynamic relationship (or covenant) of God's response to the lamentations of the oppressed by freeing them from captivity, and humankind's response of justice in human relations. The Decalogue can be found in Exodus 20:2-17 and Deuteronomy 5:6-21 with the later Deuteronomy version differing slightly from the earlier Exodus version.

Jan Jans has some interesting observations to make about how these texts differ.[1] For example, the later Deuteronomy no longer views the neighbour's wife as mere property but as having a status prior to the listing of household possessions. By not coveting one's neighbour's wife one pays proper respect not solely to the neighbour but to the wife too. She becomes if not a person of equal dignity with the male, at least something other than male property and something other than an object of the (male) gaze.

In both the Decalogue accounts there are strong commands to keep the Sabbath. In Exodus this is justified on the basis of God's mammoth work of creation: that the Lord created the world in six days and rested on the seventh and therefore blessed and made holy the Sabbath. As people made in God's image and likeness, this patterning on the basis of God's actions pays respect to the Lord.

In Deuteronomy the passage differs and the same command is justified on a different basis. A concern for the human person is inserted into the text. This time the concern is for the manservant and maidservant. All must rest, including the traveller, in order to ensure that the servants are allowed their day off too. And the justification? Remember that you too were once a servant, in bondage in Egypt. This is a sort of appeal to the golden rule: do unto others as you would have done unto you. Remember also that the Lord God delivered you from this servile state. All the more reason to keep the command.

In Deuteronomy one sees the emergence of the view that obedience to God's law is not about obedience for obedience's sake. Commands that appear arbitrary or disconnected from the wellbeing of persons are given an added humanistic dimension by the insertion of concern for the lowly: the woman and the servant.

But, as Jan Jans indicates, more can be said about the commandment about Sabbath observance. All four Gospels carry accounts of Jesus disregarding the Sabbath law for some compelling reason.

In Mark 2:23-28 it arises from Jesus' disciples plucking and eating heads of grain as they walked through the fields on the Sabbath. Jesus defends them to the Pharisees, replying that David also broke the Sabbath to eat the temple bread when he and his friends were hungry. 'The Sabbath was made for man, not man for the Sabbath,' he says. As Jesus enters the synagogue (3:1-6) the Pharisees follow him and wonder whether he will attempt to heal the man with a withered hand. Before Jesus heals him, he asks the Pharisees angrily whether it is lawful to do good or evil on the Sabbath, whether one should save life or kill?

In Matthew 12:1-13 the story is the same except Jesus cites Hosea 6:6: 'I desire mercy not sacrifice.' In Luke 6:1-6 these events are repeated. Later in chapter 13 of Luke he heals a woman bent over – to the anger of the Pharisees – and in chapter 14 in the house of a Pharisee he asks them whether it is lawful to heal on the Sabbath before curing the man with dropsy. A similar healing story, of the man born blind, is in John chapter 9.

Jesus' examples illustrate that laws should serve persons, rather than simply uphold ideals. In the concrete situations in which people find themselves, the values that lie within the ruling must be teased out and promoted as best as possible. In the case of the Sabbath law it achieves a dual purpose. It pays homage to the Lord God who has done great things for the people. It also guarantees a day of rest that is genuinely healing and good for persons. But proper reverence for the Sabbath does not include actions that let humans or animals suffer. According to Jesus it is right and proper to water your cattle or pull them from danger on the Sabbath.

The Decalogue as Mediations of Love of God and Neighbour
The Decalogue can only be properly understood as mediations of love of God and neighbour: as attempts to spell out what love of God and neighbour, means in practice. This was appreciated at the time that the *Catechism of the Catholic Church* was compiled. In the *Catechism* the section on morality is

therefore divided up into two chief sections: the first chapter is based on love of God (commandments 1-3), the second chapter on love of neighbour (commandments 4-10).

Of course, a list of commands can seem overly negative and demoralising compared with a list of positive precepts. For this reason, moral theologian, Kevin Kelly, at the time the Catechism was published in 1994, wrote out the Ten Commandments in terms of ten positive values as a means of countering the negative effects of a list of 'do nots'. These are listed in his book *From A Parish Base*,[2] and the reader may like to look to see how they offer a much more open and creative way of expressing the human response to love of God and neighbour.

A Liberation Theology Approach to HIV/AIDS

There is a strong liberation dimension to Christianity. At the beginning of Jesus' ministry he announces his life's project in the synagogue in Nazareth: 'The Spirit of the Lord is upon me, because he has anointed me to preach good news to the poor. He has sent me to proclaim release to the captives and recovering of sight to the blind, to set at liberty those who are oppressed, to proclaim the acceptable year of the Lord.' (Lk 4:18-19). In this speech, Luke has Jesus quoting from the prophet Isaiah (Is 61:1-2). Indeed the whole of Jesus' ministry can be viewed as one of liberating people from sin, healing the sick and repairing brokenness. It is given classical expression in Matthew's sermon on the mount (Mt 5:7) and Luke's sermon on the plain (Lk 6). It is clear that the priorities of the reign of God are the concerns of the sick and hungry before the comfortable and wealthy.

The Old Testament is also pervaded by this theme of liberation: not just in Isaiah. The exodus story of God's deliverance of the Hebrews from slavery in Egypt forms the backdrop to the Ten Commandments and is constantly invoked in Deuteronomy as a means of reminding the Hebrew people of their duties of concern for the weak. At the same time, the Genesis story of humankind's fall from grace illustrates the shadow side of the human desire for freedom, establishing the inherent abuse of humankind's gift of freedom. There is a grace-resistant dimension to the human condition. We lack holiness. These two strands – humankind's need for liberation and its tendency to abuse freedom – were treated at Vatican II in the landmark 1965 *Pastoral Constitution on the Church in the Modern World* (also known by its Latin title *Gaudium et Spes*).

Gaudium et Spes (among many other things) describes humankind's abuse of freedom from the beginning of history, the heart's inclination to wrongdoing, the disordered state of human relations, and the inability to liberate oneself from this state without divine help. However, it is not just individual sin that the document acknowledges. The social character of sin is acknowledged too. Humans are born into and conditioned by their sinful surrounds. There is systemic and structural injustice, political and economic corruption that distorts human relations. Sin is a condition or state rather than mere act, in which the whole social fabric is infected. To that extent, we are all sinners, but at the same time we are also all victims of sin.

To renew our relationship with our creator God and become truly free we – who are all living in sin – are called to *metanoia* – conversion of heart and life. At the same time *Gaudium et Spes* powerfully establishes God's relationship with humanity in terms of a hope-inspiring covenant relationship of enduring love (rather than as distant law-giver and judge) that calls people to humanise their world.

Since Vatican II there has been a major shift in theological perspective towards a more liberating approach that has recovered a sense of the good news of the Gospel. Theology has come to be seen as not just a search for the truth, but a truth that will make people free. It has a liberation dimension because it is aimed at understanding what is good for human persons.

Previously, Catholic theology, rather than affirming persons, could seem impoverished, scholastic and life-denying. Catholic theology pre-Vatican II seemed to glide high over human affairs, missing the contextual features of the landscape below, and it therefore appeared to be something that could be divorced from ordinary Catholic lives in all their diversity and complexity. The contrast may be envisaged as follows:

A life-denying theology ...	A liberating theology ...
God as judge	God as encourager and enabler
Moral living = dos and don'ts	Moral living = being and becoming
Goodness = obedience to rules	Goodness = embodying values and virtues
The Church is a hierarchy	The Church is a discipleship of equals

When theologians applied the insights of *Gaudium et Spes* to the local Church context in Latin America with its conditions of poverty and injustice it gave rise to what became known as 'liberation theology' which quickly spread to other oppressed groups who applied the same fundamental principles to their own situation of marginalisation and communal struggle for justice, giving rise to black theology, Asian liberation theology, feminist theology and gay theology. Without doubt, liberation approaches have been among the most influential theologies since Vatican II.

Key Aspects of Liberation Theology
The key elements of liberation theology seek to make sense of the two approaches to freedom already outlined in *Gaudium et*

Spes. Firstly, humankind's propensity to abuse its gift of freedom and shirk its responsibility. Secondly, humanity's resultant need for liberation from this network of sin through God's loving initiative.

Liberation theology is concerned with the *humanum* and transformation of this world as a means of bringing about the Kingdom of God (rather than seeing it as something that can be deferred until the next life). The growth of the Kingdom of God takes place in human history through liberation in all its forms. God's action in history (especially through Christ) has been to bring liberation to the oppressed. Social analysis of the human situation allows the many instances of injustice to be recognised, acknowledged and understood. This in turn leads to an awakening or conscientisation which leads to a prioritising on the basis of those most in need (the preferential option for the poor) and a siding with the marginalised, disenfranchised, alienated and oppressed in an expression of solidarity – as the biblical witness so strongly attests.

The Strengths of Liberation Theology

Liberation theology is successful because it shows that the Gospel message has the power to transform people's lives and mobilise work for justice and liberation. It incarnates the best theology of Vatican II. It responds meaningfully in a practical and theological way to the universal problem of unjust and avoidable human suffering. It combines Scripture, doctrinal theology and the social teachings of the Church in ways not previously achieved.

Prior to Vatican II, social teachings were largely premised on the insights of philosophy and human reason rather than the Bible and theology; on Catholic interpretations of natural law. Liberation theology is therefore a theologically rich way of presenting the Christian vision of the world. And it is prophetic

– it has uncomfortable words for comfortable Christians about our shared responsibility and lack of concern for the needy.

Liberation theology has subsequently been re-appropriated by the Vatican in its social teaching in the writings of John Paul and the Congregation for the Doctrine of the Faith. The margins have changed the centre. The focus of Catholic Social Teaching has shifted from its nineteenth-century concern over the economic conditions of the poor in the industrial revolution in the west to the conditions of those in the southern hemisphere. Few can deny the powerful advocacy for the poor and oppressed by the Catholic Church and its action for a more humane society that has built on the Catholic social tradition since the so-called Worker's encyclical *Rerum Novarum* (1891) and combined it with a more keen biblical witness (especially in the writings of John Paul II) and firmer Gospel foundations.

Liberation Theology in the Context of HIV/AIDS

When applied to the devastating consequences of the HIV/AIDS pandemic a liberation theology approach attempts to incarnate a Gospel response confident that Jesus, in his life and ministry, was closest not to the morally upright but to those whose lives were in collapse. Liberation theology approaches to HIV analyse the unjust structures that are at play in the spread of the pandemic and turn to the liberating good news of the Gospel to address these sinful causes, to provide care and advocacy and to empower those laid low by its impact. The process of liberation is at three interrelated levels:

• Liberation in the political, social, cultural and economic sphere, to deliver people from those factors that increase vulnerability to infection. For those familiar with the model employed by Enda McDonagh and Ann Smith in the excellent *The Reality of HIV/AIDS*, this corresponds to the shallow and deep roots of the HIV problem tree.

- Personal liberation in which those affected and infected by the disease rediscover and maintain their dignity and self-belief in the face of the disease and in the face of discrimination and stigma.
- Liberation from sin. This is surely the most challenging behaviour change required, not least because there are powerful and often oppressive forces that reduce human freedom and that make change difficult, personally threatening and at times even impossible. Conversion (*metanoia*) in these circumstances cannot be anything other than incremental, show regression as well as advance, and occur only with the accompaniment of all the pastoral resources that a community and Church has at its disposal. It is inconceivable that Catholics affected by and infected with HIV should be prevented from drawing nourishment from the sacramental life of the Church at such a vital time.

A liberation theology approach can communicate God's undying love for each of us, God's immediate forgiveness of those who express sorrow and remorse for wrongdoing, and the hope and faith that death, suffering, illness, loss and failure are not the end. The Gospels end not in utter abjection with the scandal of the cross, but in new life and empowerment as the Spirit descends as promised spreading its healing wisdom far and wide. In this *kairos* time we must seize the opportunity rather than hide in fear.

The irruption of the poor that emerged in Latin America and other colonised lands is now also an irruption of those living with HIV, previously ignored or omitted from pastoral ministry. Absent, now present, revealing the wounds of Christ and the wounded Church. Afflicted but no longer silent. The unjust sufferings and hopes of those affected by and infected with the virus speak out to us and evangelise us – calling us back to the urgency of the Gospel message.

Only by denouncing the injustices of HIV will the Church offer a prophetic witness. Thus, alongside such work, a liberation theology approach to HIV will be engaged in conscientisation – educating those at risk and educating wider society to end the discrimination, stigma, and take up the challenge of responding to the pandemic.

Liberation Theology Presupposes the Liberation of Theology

Despite the prophetic witness and untiring work of many Catholics committed to combating the pandemic, it is clear that some parts of the worldwide Catholic Church (composed of over 1 billion adherents) have not fully incarnated this liberative Vatican II vision.

On the ground, both clergy and lay people are living with medieval manifestations of Catholicism that are obstructing efforts to fight the pandemic. For example, notions that women are subordinate to males and should passively comply with or obey male authority, that disease is divine punishment for wrongdoing, or that innocent victims of exploitation are guilty of mortal sin and doomed to hell fire if they take measures to avoid infection. These horrific manifestations – while found within Catholicism – are simply not Catholic.

At the same time, some members of the Church laity and hierarchy have been blind to or even complicit with injustice on the grounds of gender and sexual orientation despite the fact that these are expressly counter to Catholic teaching. At the level of the Church as institution, the doers of theology and those who formulate theology in Church teachings are not infrequently operating out of an understanding of Church and world that is at odds with the Vatican II vision.

Furthermore, the Church's moral teachings and appeals to Scripture are being misapplied when they are proposed in ways that are harmful to persons. In other words, commandments are being invoked without the overarching interpretative framework of the dual love command (for God and neighbour) and without attention to Jesus' lived example (such as on Sabbath observance). Sadly, traditional institutional theology as it emerges from Rome can all too often speak a theological language that is more congenial to the superstition, ignorance, fear, blind obedience and monarchical authority of Catholic medievalism.

In the same way that the visual model of a problem tree can help to portray the causes and effects of the pandemic, a similar effort could be drawn up to show how certain ignorance, misapplication of Church teaching, misapplication of Scripture, pastoral insensitivity, fear of the magisterium and Bishops, bigotry and prejudice about Catholic teaching (some of which have deeper theological roots than others) are increasing vulnerability to infection and hampering development work. The effects of these distortions (the branches of the problem tree) are clear. New infections, more deaths, alienation from the Church, loss of Catholic credibility and so on.

The Catholic Church has a liberative theological vision that can ground pastoral and development responses to HIV/AIDS. The problem and challenge is making this good news of the Gospel known and sensitively countering the ignorance, prejudice and misunderstanding.

Note

1 Jan Jans, 'Neither punishment nor reward: Divine Gratuitousness and Moral Order' *Concilium*, 4, (2004), pp. 83-92.

2 Kevin T. Kelly, *From a Parish Base: Essays in Moral and Pastoral Theology* (London: DLT, 1999).

Reading

Stuart C. Bate OMI (ed.) *Responsibility in a Time of AIDS: A Pastoral Response by Catholic Theologians and AIDS Activists in Southern Africa* (Pietermaritzburg, South Africa: Cluster Publications, 2003).

James F. Keenan SJ (ed.) *Catholic Ethicists on HIV/AIDS Prevention* (New York: Continuum, 2000).

Kevin T. Kelly, *New Directions In Sexual Ethics* (London: Geoffrey Chapman, 1998).

———— *From a Parish Base: Essays in Moral and Pastoral Theology* (London: DLT, 1999).

Ann Smith and Enda McDonagh, *The Reality of HIV/AIDS* (Dublin: Veritas, 2003).